Head to Head

GREAT GOLF DEBATES

Jeremy Ellwood and Fergus Bisset are single-figure handicappers with a passion, nay, obsession for the game.

Jeremy is *Golf Monthly*'s associate editor, contributing to a wide range of the magazine's editorial content from travel and course reviews, to in-depth features and player profiles. He has also written for *The Independent*, *The Mail on Sunday*'s *Live* magazine and even the mighty ebay! His game is based very much on 'how many' rather than 'how', and the autobiographical slant to the 'scrambling' argument in the 'consistency vs scrambling' debate within these pages will be instantly obvious to anyone who's ever played with him.

Fergus is *Golf Monthly*'s contributing editor. A freelance writer, he's been working with the magazine for almost four years. He has also written for *Total Golf*, *The Mail on Sunday*'s *Live* magazine, *Sky* magazine and *Square Mile* magazine. Hailing from Aberdeenshire in Scotland and having attended University in St Andrews, golf runs freely through his veins. Fergus has little time for anything other than serious medal play off the back tees and is widely regarded as one of the unluckiest golfers to have ever wielded a club in anger.

Head to Head

GREAT GOLF DEBATES

JEREMY ELLWOOD and FERGUS BISSET

Illustrated by
RUPERT BESLEY

BIRLINN

First published in 2009 by
Birlinn Limited
West Newington House
10 Newington Road
Edinburgh
EH9 1QS

www.birlinn.co.uk

ISBN13: 978 1 84158 777 6
ISBN10: 1 84158 777 X

British Library Cataloguing-in-Publication Data
A catalogue record for this book is available from the British Library

Designed and typeset by Iolaire Typesetting, Newtonmore
Printed and bound by CPI, Mackays of Chatham

CONTENTS

CONTENTS

FOREWORD

Debate, argument, rant or ruck; call it what you will, but here, I believe, we have the very fuel of an interesting life. Throw in romance, love, family, at least two loyal pals and a decent Petit Chablis and we may actually be on to something slightly important.

'Jezza' (Jeremy is his formal name only) and Fergus (if he has an informal name then it is probably 'Too Good At Golf', an old Sioux/Scottish moniker I understand) have called this book GREAT GOLF DEBATES but in truth it is nothing of the sort. Neither should it be. Debating stuff is all very well if you need some light relief after spending a hard day contemplating something heavy and vaguely academic at Oxford or Cambridge but for the rest of us a good, old fashioned, screaming disagreement is what releases the calming stuff inside our fevered bodies. This Messrs Ellwood and Bisset have achieved.

Personally I find this book irritating but the only reason it's irritating is that it is so enjoyable and that I didn't think of doing it myself. Quite why I didn't come up with the idea is beyond me. I often lose my arguments with myself although my psychiatrist, somewhat encouragingly, says this is something I should grow out of. Either that or I will fall off my perch raging against the dying of the light. At least this should please Dylan Thomas, if no-one else.

Whatever, reading the enclosed chapters made me think of what my own opinion was on each of the subjects the chaps have chosen to lock horns over. As each obviously takes an opposing view on topics that range from the bleeding obvious (Woods or Nicklaus) through the esoteric (carrying versus trolleying) and on to the, frankly, bizarre (50-yard bunker shot versus flop shot off a bare lie (as if)) I found myself constantly in agreement with one of them and therefore reinforced in my ongoing belief that I always know best.

What is also true is that golf, more than most games, does throw up these moments of high disagreement. Everyone has a favourite course or player or clubhouse bar, everyone is passionate about these things as well as many others and it is also my experience that the average golfer holds more entrenched opinions than a career politician confronted by an expenses form.

The authors display this admirable quality superbly well. Reassuringly, there is no give or take and each often seems to make a compelling case for his opinion only to lose out – at least in my opinion – to the opponent's take on things. This is how it should be. Life isn't fair and debating shouldn't be either. Not a bad idea for a debate in itself. As a book, this tome not only makes a brilliant doorstop, it actually encourages the reader to think for him/herself. Yes, that's correct, I am not going to debate feminism here.

The following words will happily fill in those tedious hours between disconsolately finishing an especially poor round and starting the next disappointment. Jezza and Fergus tell me they think they have written a really, really good book. Just this once, I am not prepared to argue with them.

Bill Elliott
June 2009

INTRODUCTION

Former US Ryder Cup player Gardner Dickinson was once heard to remark: 'They say golf is like life, but don't believe them. Golf is more complicated than that.' Any golf enthusiast reading this will now have a wry smile on their face, as Dickinson really hit the nail on the head there.

Golf is all consuming. There's a seemingly bottomless pool of information to absorb on the sport, everything from the rules to the technical specifications of the latest equipment. Then there are the innumerable dilemmas the game throws up – where to play, how to play, who to play with, what to play with . . . The options are endless and decision-making causes all golfers to be pretty opinionated when it comes to 'their' game and how they like to enjoy it.   This is why golf is the greatest game. Everyone can enjoy it at their own level and strive to get exactly what they want from it. Some will aim to play to par, others to break 100. Some will aim to take less than three hours to get round, others to take less than three air shots during their round. Some will be looking forward to the post-round debrief in the clubhouse, others will be heading straight for the driving range to iron out the kinks in their game before another battle against the links the following day.

The point is, there's often no right or wrong way in golf – though most will be able to provide convincing arguments to support their methods and opinions. Go into clubhouses the length and breadth of this country and you'll find debates raging on everything from the best destination for a golfing break in Wales to whether the club pairs championship should be contested using a fourball or four-somes format.

Almost all sportspeople are argumentative; it goes hand in hand with competition. How often do you hear footballers shouting, 'He was clearly offside, ref!', or tennis players crying out, 'That ball was on the line. I saw chalk dust!' But, as the rules of golf are so definitive, competitors can't really dispute decisions on the course. The ball is either out of bounds or it's not; the putt either ended up in the bottom of the cup or it didn't. So to satisfy our quarrelsome streaks we must direct our squabbles elsewhere. Should the greens be a touch faster? Are bladed irons superior to cavity backs? Is it preferable to hit a fade or a draw? There's a good deal to get your teeth into.

In this book we've picked 45 potentially contentious issues – some serious, some distinctly light-hearted – and tried to approach each in an impartial way. We haven't necessarily done this from our personal standpoints; we've just thought about the pros and cons to each side of each argument and put them down on paper.

It's by no means an instructional manual, though there are a few chapters that might provide some guidance during those traumatic moments on the links when the debate raging in your brain shifts into top gear and sensible decision making becomes a rather unlikely prospect.

You'll probably agree with some of what's said over the next 200 pages, and possibly disagree with a lot of it too. But, whether you read a chapter nodding in appreciation or find yourself yelling, 'What the hell are these idiots talking about?', you'll hopefully have some extra ammunition to shoot from the hip with next time clubhouse chat strays onto one of the debates covered here.

Jeremy Ellwood
Fergus Bisset
August 2009

1
TIGER WOODS vs JACK NICKLAUS

Who is golf's greatest-ever player? Most authorities on the game now have it narrowed down to these two names. Both have struck fear into the hearts of opponents and dominated world golf during long tenures at the pinnacle of the game. But which man sits at the top of the pile?

TIGER WOODS

The contention has to end. Tiger Woods is the greatest golfer of all time. He has totally dominated the sport since turning professional in 1996. He has the rest of today's top players trailing deferentially in his wake. His ball striking is unmatched and his short game would rival Seve's in his prime. He keeps himself in peak physical condition and possesses an incredible ability to win even when playing poorly. His aggressive style has influenced a new generation of golfers and his mental approach is the benchmark to which all other pros aspire. This golfing demigod eclipses any player, even Jack Nicklaus.

Some stats: Tiger Woods won six US amateur titles (three junior, three senior), Jack Nicklaus won two. Between the ages of 20 and 29 Tiger won 46 PGA Tour events, Nicklaus took just 30. Woods had ten majors before reaching the age of 30, Nicklaus had seven. Those who argue Jack is still the greatest rely resolutely and obstinately on a single statistic: his 18 majors compared to Tiger's 14. Well, Tiger is only 33 years old. The Golden Bear won his last major aged 46 – the 1986 Masters. If Tiger continues at his present rate, he'll have 30 by then. So it's Jack – one stat (soon to be overtaken) – vs Tiger – every other stat going.

As an important aside, the number of majors won should not be the sole barometer for deciding golfing ability. If it were, then we'd have to say that Todd Hamilton, with one major title, is a superior golfer to Colin Montgomerie with none; or that supremely talented Sergio Garcia cannot be considered a finer player than 1953 US PGA Champion Walter Burkemo. It's preposterous. The main point is that nobody has ever *played* golf as well as Tiger Woods. Put the Tiger of 2009 against the Jack Nicklaus of 1972 and Woods would win.

Professional golf has never had more strength in depth than at present. There are hundreds of exceptionally talented players across the globe. Places on the main tours are contested with increasing ferocity and only the best of the best will be able to compete as regulars on either the European or PGA tours. Each week anybody in the field has a realistic chance of lifting the trophy come Sunday afternoon. The fact that Tiger can consistently stand above the crowd is testament to his superiority as a golfer. Yes, Nicklaus had rivals in Palmer, Player, Miller and Watson, but he didn't have to contend against hordes of top-class challengers like those Tiger fends off week after week.

Woods is abnormally consistent. He's only missed the cut five times in his entire career. He's only missed two cuts in majors and one of them came at the 2006 US Open after six weeks off following the death of his father. Jack Nicklaus had missed the cut in six majors by the time he was 30, and had missed 30 major cuts by the end of his career.

The weight of evidence is overwhelming. It's Woods by a five-shot margin.

JACK NICKLAUS

Woods or Nicklaus, Nicklaus or Woods? Since Tiger's 2006 USPGA victory hoisted him ahead of Walter Hagen into outright second place on the all-time major victories list, the debate as to who is the greatest golfer to have graced the world's fairways has really hotted up. He now trails Jack 18–14 with regard to golf's four major championships, with apparently many years in hand to eclipse the Golden Bear's seemingly impregnable record. If he maintains his major strike rate, he'll be there in next to no time.

But whether he gets there sooner, later or never, for many Nicklaus will always remain the greatest. Golfing greatness extends beyond just major success – and indeed playing records of any kind – though if you want to add substantial weight to Jack's playing claims, just ponder this: on top of those 18 major victories he also finished second 19 times, in the top three 46 times, the top five 56 times and the top ten 73 times in golf's big four events. Then there's the small matter of 111 professional victories worldwide to consider. And of course those 18 major victories are already in the bag while Tiger still has work to do.

But what else sets the Golden Bear apart from the Tiger in golf's greatness stakes? Firstly, Tiger was being groomed for golfing excellence by an enthusiastic father from the age of just two; Jack didn't start playing till he was ten, giving him perhaps a slightly more rounded early childhood. Then, after one particular youthful club-throwing tantrum, Jack was told by his father that if he hurled just one more club in anger it would be the last time he played golf. He never threw a club again. Tiger is still prone to the occasional club toss – and they come back down to earth with a slightly distasteful clang from the lofty perch of undisputed world number one and an influential role model to golfing youngsters everywhere.

Jack, as far as we're aware, never spat on the golf course; Tiger does, and it's a habit that's totally unnecessary in a non-aerobic sport. And finally, Jack's celebrations – save for nearly decapitating the orange-clad Doug Sanders with his putter at St Andrews in 1970 – were always appropriately under control; Tiger's post-shot celebrations sometimes verge on the overly aggressive.

Some of this may sound like nit-picking, and much of the way Tiger conducts himself is perhaps symptomatic of our modern times as much as anything. In many ways he does extraordinarily well considering the 24/7 'goldfish bowl' world he inhabits. He can't even pick his nose without someone wanting to get a picture or write about it.

Tiger may well get there on the major front, although the ferocity with which he has been swinging the club from a tender age may herald further physical problems as he gets older to add to the knee that required surgery again in 2008. But even if he does make it, for many he will never be as great an all-round package as Jack. It's certainly hard to imagine Tiger as a past-his-prime, slightly pot-bellied 46-year-old in a pair of bad trousers notching up one final fairy-tale major success, as Nicklaus did in the 1986 Masters.

2

LINKS vs PARKLAND COURSES

Links courses are a little like Marmite – you either love them or loathe them. And manicured parkland courses, a source of inspiration to some, just leave others cold. But who is the real winner in the battle between Windswept-on-Sea Golf Links and Towering Oaks Golf and Country Club?

LINKS

The smell of salt and gorse lingers on the ever-present breeze, the real world seems distant as the call of songbirds rings through the crisp seaside air and the rushes rustle atop the towering sand dunes.

The sun glints off your ball as you prepare to launch it down the firm narrow fairway stretching away in front of you. This is golf as it should be. Our great game originated by the sea and the links remains the place where the sport can be enjoyed in its purest form.

Britain is famous across the world for its golf courses. We are blessed with over 2,500 of them and people travel from the four corners to sample the golfing delights our country has to offer. But the majority of these tourists skirt the perimeter of Great Britain, seldom venturing inland. Why? It's because tedious and repetitive parkland courses can be found all over the world, but true links are confined to Britain. They are historic, captivating, testing and unique. From Nairn in the north to Rye in the south, from Brancaster in the east to Saunton in the west, ask anybody with knowledge and understanding of golf and they'll tell you Britain's best courses are to be found by the sea.

The UK's grand old links still represent the pinnacle of course design. Many modern architects strive to emulate their bunkering, plateau greens, raised tees and natural contours. These coastal tracks provide a true test of the golfer's ability. An impressive arsenal of shots and a vivid imagination are required to return a good score. The links golfer will be master of the knocked-down iron into the wind, the chip and run, the punched 3-wood and the long putt from off the green.

Striking a ball cleanly and crisply from firm seaside turf is one of the most difficult golfing skills to master. When it's executed correctly the feeling is hard to beat. Chopping around a muddy field somewhere in middle England simply does not compare. The parkland golfer will play a high ball from the tee to the green. He'll play lofted pitches aiming to stop the ball by the pin and his technique will hardly vary.

One of the great things about links courses is they're playable all year round. In mid January when the average parkland course is totally waterlogged and play is confined to winter tees and temporary greens, the links are still playing their full length to firm, well-running putting surfaces. On days when there's a hard frost inland, the seaside can often be ice-free.

Consider this. Where would you rather be holing out to win a golf tournament? On the windswept 18th at Royal Birkdale after winning a ferocious battle against the elements, the firm ground, the treacherous bunkers and the uncompromising rough? Or the last at Forest of Arden after playing every hole in the same monotonous fashion and plodding home uneventfully? There's no contest: the links wins on all counts.

PARKLAND COURSES

Show me a golfer who claims to have had fun stepping off a links course on a brutal day, having been buffeted to within an inch of his golfing life and bearing a scorecard that's been ripped to shreds both physically and metaphorically, and I'll show you a highly accomplished liar and potentially brilliant spin doctor.

Britain is famed for being a 'green and pleasant' land, is it not? Lines of neat hedgerows separating field after field of lush vegetation. But you certainly wouldn't get that impression setting foot on one of our coastline's bleak and barren links, where the very idea of greenness is frowned upon and the whole emphasis seems to be on making you, the golfer, look as silly as possible.

On the links you'll encounter almost unplayably firm, tight fairways and greens, undulations and humps designed to test your patience to the limit by kicking your ball unfairly into the often punishing rough, and bunkers so devilishly deep they're even capable of inflicting humiliating suffering on the world's best, just like the old Hamlet ads. Happiness is definitely not hitting two decent shots into a green, watching your ball sweep away viciously into a cavernous greenside bunker, taking six hacks to finally extricate yourself and then three-putting with ease on a crisp roller-coaster putting surface.

Add in the kind of wind that makes your ball dance around like a hyperactive Michael Flatley and it's easy to see why many golfers prefer to seek shelter inland far from the crashing waves and howling breeze.

Holes bordered by beautiful flowering shrubs wending their way through lines of mature trees with, perhaps, the occasional well-placed pond to negotiate – these are the ones that really set the golfing pulse racing. And unlike the unpredictable firmness of the links, parkland greens are usually willing to receive a well-struck ball, so you can even take luck out of the equation on your approach play. Good shots will be rewarded.

Parkland courses will make you a better player too, for a couple of reasons. Firstly, you're not constantly tinkering with your swing and set-up to counter the effects of the wind, or forever trying punch shots that you don't really have in your armoury. A tough day on a links can destroy your rhythm for many a round to come. Then, although there is undoubtedly trouble away from the short grass on a links, the visual frame of reference from the tee is often not intimidatingly claustrophobic. Stand on the tee of a tight, pine-lined dog-leg at a Wentworth-style track, however, and you'll soon discover how straight you really hit the ball and how well your game stands up under the most severe visual pressure.

Through a long-standing association with The Open Championship, links courses may at first glance appear to form the backbone of Britain's golfing heritage. But is it not the lush beauty of our parkland layouts that fits in more comfortably with our nation's reputation for greenness and pleasantness?

3

SHANK vs
AIR SHOT

The primary objective of golf is to move a ball into a distant hole in as few strokes as possible. With this in mind the air shot would appear to be the worst thing a golfer can do – a stroke gone but no progress made. There is, however, a contender for worst effort. It comes in the shape of the dreaded shank.

AIR SHOT

If ever one of these debates represented Hobson's choice then this is it. For who in their right mind would ever want to hit – or not hit in the case of the air shot – either of these two horror strokes? And is it really possible to argue against the shank – that most alarming of efforts when the ball comes into contact with the neck of the club, sending it scurrying away at near right angles to the intended target?

In terms of your scorecard, perhaps not, as the air shot will at least leave you facing the same shot again from exactly the same place, while the shank could see you stymied in the deep dark forest, apologising profusely for nearly taking the captain's head off on an adjacent green, or quite possibly lying out of bounds.

But we need to see the wider picture here. To clarify a little, an air shot is only that one where you make a full-blooded swing only to miss the little dimpled sphere completely, with club typically passing either above or to the player's side of it. An air shot is *not* that one when the ball is sitting up so much in the rough that, in trying to be too cute, you slide your club right underneath it and miss it altogether on the low side. That is something else – a grass shot or whatever you want to call it. An air shot is simply what it says – one where the only thing your club head strikes is the invisible mix of nitrogen, oxygen and carbon dioxide that envelops us.

The air shot is a black-and-white admission that your swing cannot yet guarantee contact of at least some kind. It is, if you like, a non-golfer's worst shot. The shank, on the other hand – sometimes rather fancifully described as the closest bad shot to a perfect one – is very much a golfer's miss, with the club coming back into the ball just fractionally outside the ideal line.

It is a shot played by a real golfer whose set-up or swing plane has got just a fraction out of sync, and is usually only a passing affliction – albeit a highly damaging one for both scorecard and morale. You will never see a professional or good amateur hit a true air shot; you will sometimes see them hit the odd 'Sherman', 'J. Arthur' or 'Lucy Locket' – self-preserving terms adopted by golfers desperate to avoid using the actual word.

The reality is that after a shank you should be able to look yourself in the mirror and say, 'I've just hit a horror shot, but it's only a temporary blip – I am a real golfer.' A similarly honest analysis of an air shot would have to be, 'Oh well, I've still got a bit of work to do to crack this swing thing – it seems I'm not yet a real golfer.' Hobson's choice it may be, but wouldn't you prefer the former?

SHANK

In the same way actors never mention *Macbeth* (they call it 'the Scottish play'), golfers should never utter the dreaded word 'shank'. From here on it'll be referred to by one of its many euphemisms.

No shot strikes such fear into the heart of golfers and nothing is more debilitating than contracting a bout of the terrifying 'J. Arthurs'. Every iron shot could spell complete disaster. Like a ninja assassin under cover of darkness, the 'Tom Hank' appears from nowhere and could attack at any time. A 'Scottish shot' is just millimetres away from being a reasonable strike but, when the hosel gets involved, all hell breaks loose. You could be just 70 yards short of the green then hit a 'Lucy Locket' out of bounds or into a pond. You've then got to drop one and the chances are you'll do the same again. A good score can turn into a no-return frighteningly quickly.

Accepted, an air shot will cause embarrassment. But the red face will quickly disappear when you fire the next one 200 yards down the fairway, get on the green with your third, then sink the putt for par. The problem with the 'Sherman' is that it seldom comes as a singleton. You're generally afflicted by a dose of them and you'll be shouting 'Fore right' before you've even stood up to the ball. Alternatively, you'll start hitting massive pulls in a desperate attempt to avoid the hosel – these can be equally destructive. The psychological damage inflicted by a severe case of the 'Gordon Banks' can be permanent. People have quit the game because of acute cases.

An air shot happens when you come up on the ball. It's fairly easily avoided: just make a slow and solid swing, keeping your eye on the ball, and you'll make contact with it. Apparently there are 13 separate ways to hit a 'Shabba Rank', so they're notoriously difficult to fix. A 'touch of Scottish' can affect players of all abilities, even the top pros. Ian Poulter suffered a minor affliction a couple of years ago and Darren Clarke has been caught on camera producing a 'socket rocket'.

This is what makes the 'Davy Crockett' so scary. No matter how good you get at the game you're not immune. For a reasonable golfer the air shot will be a complete freak occurrence, something playing partners will laugh at and recount with mirth in the clubhouse. Hit a shank and your playing partners will look to the ground. They won't discuss it to your face, but will mutter behind your back, 'He's got the J. Arthurs.' You'll be a condemned man.

Here's the choice. Take an air shot, laugh riotously with your playing partners, then blast the next one towards the green. Or hit an 'unmentionable', thereby planting the seed of doubt in your mind, leave the course psychologically crippled and lose your game completely for five years. It's a fairly easy decision.

4

MEDAL vs STABLEFORD

Next time you sign up for a competition, what format are you hoping it will be – medal, where every shot counts and there's no margin for significant error if your sights are set on the prize table, or Stableford, where a slightly more lenient format allows for the odd hiccup along the way without completely dashing your hopes?

MEDAL

The medal round is golf's purest challenge. You'll find 'record a great medal score' high on the must-achieve list of the majority of true golf lovers. With every shot counting it's this format that separates the wheat from the chaff. Medal play identifies the best golfers from club level right up to the professional game.

A solid medal round requires precise planning and careful strategy. The good medal player will be patient. He'll know when to take opportunities and when to play it safe. As a result a carefully crafted medal round will give great satisfaction, as well as confirming golfing prowess. Inconsistent players who have the odd good hole can still score well in Stableford, but these golfers often can't construct a good round. To win a medal you must play 18 decent holes and can't afford any significant errors. It must be remembered that the ability to achieve this is not the sole preserve of the low handicapper. There's no reason a high handicapper can't return good medal scores. He simply has to know how to make his shots count. If he's receiving 18 strokes there's no need for him to try and carry the pond on stroke index 1 in a desperate attempt to make birdie. He can lay up, pitch on and try to save par. If he does it's a bonus, if not he's still in the game.

When playing in medal competition you're using the scoring system favoured in professional competitions week in, week out. Can you imagine if the R&A decided to make The Open a Stableford competition? When Jean van de Velde lost his mind on the 18th at Carnoustie in 1999 it wouldn't have mattered. He'd already have accumulated enough points to take the title after the 17th. It would have been even more ridiculous than his stream-wading antics.

This is one of the principal arguments against Stableford. Someone can win a competition despite having an abomination at one, or even more than one, hole. It's not fair for a steady competitor to be beaten by one more erratic than Wayne Rooney's temper. If someone has a complete blow-up and takes a 17 on a hole they do not deserve to win anything.

Stableford has its place: the corporate outing or charity day, for instance. But you'll never see significant events decided using this distorted version of the game. For the connoisseur, medal play is the only way. The Club Championship will never be Stableford, men's Opens are not Stableford, the Brabazon Trophy is not Stableford and the US Masters is not Stableford. The reason being, all these competitions strive to find the best golfer and Stableford doesn't necessarily do this. If you record 36 Stableford points it suggests you've played to your handicap. But you might not have done. Four nett birdies might have cancelled out two blobs on holes where you actually scored a 19 and a 25. You can't really feel like you've gone round in level par having done that. Medal play will always be superior to Stableford as the latter gives a false representation of golfing ability.

STABLEFORD

Let's get one thing straight about Stableford scoring before we launch into its merits – it is, to all intents and purposes, legalised cheating. In what other sport is it actually permitted to just ignore shots you'd rather forget? That, of course, is its beauty and key selling point. When you reach a certain figure on a hole, the scorecard stops counting, recording simply zero points rather than a number that exceeds the average England cricket score on their pitiful 2007 Ashes tour.

That's precisely why Dr Frank Barney Gorton Stableford invented the system – so one total disaster didn't have the power to wipe out an entire round. The tough par 4 2nd at Wallasey Golf Club was where he had his eureka moment, inspired by the plight of fellow golfers whose scorecards and spirits so often lay in tatters just 20 or 30 minutes into their games. The thought of them wallowing in self-pity for the next 3 hours with no hope of salvaging anything was too much for the good doctor to bear, so he set about finding a way of downgrading disasters into mere mishaps, leaving them with plenty to still play for.

The cunning legacy he left behind denies those demoralising tens and elevens the power to sap the golfing lifeblood from you by effectively turning them into sixes or sevens – depending on handicap – leaving you shots better off than in a medal. It bails inconsistent golfers out of the serious trouble they so often get themselves into, while still fully rewarding their good play. That's why average golfers love it so much more than the unyielding medal, where what you shoot is what you get – warts and all.

Of course, some would say that is also its weakness – you can play two identical rounds and end up with two very different results. But most of us want to play golf for fun rather than as some lifelong penance for the unmentionable crimes of a past life.

And it's not just about the real horror scores either. What about those irksome doubles and trebles that plunge us into a trough of despondency in a medal? Often they come at the toughest holes where we get a shot – maybe two – which means that in a Stableford we still end up with a point. Same gross score in both formats, but somehow that point gives us something to cling on to. Who hasn't at some stage found himself saying to his playing partners 'At least I still got a point there' after the kind of hole which would have resulted in hair being torn out in large clumps in a medal? The precise psychology of this remains a mystery, but it's probably a simple maths thing – one point just sounds so much better than two or three dropped shots.

So next time you're in the Liverpool area, take a moment to stop by at Wallasey Golf Club and doff your tam-o'-shanter to Dr Stableford – the man who made all our Saturday and Sunday mornings so much more enjoyable. Let's allow the great Henry Longhurst to have the final word: 'I doubt whether any single man did more to increase the pleasure of the more humble club golfer.' Quite!

5
VERY SLOW PLAY vs
VERY FAST PLAY

The curse of slow play regularly makes the headlines and is one of the game's most vexing issues. But an equally irksome, yet less reported, pace-of-play issue is caused by golfers who hound others off the course in their determination to beat the stopwatch over and above the scorecard. Who are the more irritating – the golfing tortoises or the golfing hares?

VERY SLOW PLAY

Imagine the scene – you've managed to find 4 hours in your busy schedule to nip down to the club for a swift 18 holes. You arrive at the course and feel a pang of anxiety when you see a coach parked

17

outside the clubhouse. That pang of anxiety turns into full-blown panic when you reach the 1st tee and find it occupied by the last four-ball of a group of 36 elderly Norwegian tourists. Three and a half hours later you're forced to walk off from the 13th. Rather than enjoying a few hours winding down, you've managed to work yourself into a frenzy and you leave the course far more stressed than when you arrived. Slow play is torture and takes all enjoyment out of golf.

The curse of slow play affects the sport at all levels. From the top professionals right down to society hackers it has become an epidemic. The speed of play in professional tournaments is laughable. Even playing in two-balls their rounds can often take 5 hours. Golfers like J.B. Holmes, whose pre-shot routine offers the TV viewing public the chance to make a cup of tea or pop to the shops before he actually hits the ball, set a terrible example for juniors or those starting out in the game. People are given the impression that it's acceptable to consider every shot for 5 minutes before making a swing.

The problem is, the average amateur takes 20 shots per round more than the likes of Holmes. Add 20 extra pre-shot routines and you're looking at a very long and very boring round of golf. Now throw into the mix people failing to play when ready, marking their cards while still on the green, leaving their trolleys in the wrong place, failing to let people through when they've lost a ball and walking at a snail's pace between shots. The long, boring round becomes an agonising epic.

It's almost impossible to keep your composure and continue to focus on your game when you're stuck behind a group of slow players. When you're forced to wait on every shot your mind wanders and you begin to question your club and shot selection. By the time you're finally able to hit, your brain is so muddled you've no chance of making a decent pass at it.

Slow play can affect your life outside golf – you've budgeted 3 hours for a game and told friends and family you'll be free for another activity at a set time. When that time comes and you're still standing on the 16th tee your heart sinks. You know you've let them down, your day is effectively ruined and it's all the fault of the unhurried golfers ahead.

Slow play is a scourge on our great game and must be eradicated. For those sluggish golfers (and you know who your are), next time you're dawdling your way to a four-and-a-half-hour round, have a little consideration for the players behind you. You might not have a life to get back to but some of them do.

VERY FAST PLAY

Overly fast players are more infuriating than dawdlers. There . . . it's out, no doubt leaving the old guard foaming at the mouth in these 'slow play is golf's ultimate curse' times. Of course, the golfing tortoises are immensely frustrating too, whether they're marking their scorecards on the greens or viewing putts from every conceivable angle before leaving them 8 feet short and going through the whole painful process again.

Yes, if you've taken 2½ hours to the turn and are languishing three holes adrift, clearly you're too slow and deserve to be on the receiving end of subtle and not-so-subtle hints from those following. But on most courses, 3½ hours for a three-ball is generally OK, however much some may bleat on about sub 3 hours being the norm.

It's annoying to play at an acceptable pace only for club members behind to race up behind you like the Roadrunner, constantly hounding you in a determined bid to get past. Isn't it sad that they actually get more enjoyment out of this than the game itself? 'How did you get on today, George?' 'Great – got through three groups by the 9th.' They don't putt out and race from green to tee, only ever playing half the game. They could happily slip away to clearer parts of the course if they wanted to – after all, if they're not scoring, does it really matter which holes they play? But they don't want to. They want to get one over on you.

But you may have paid good money for the privilege and understandably may wish to savour the course and, heaven forbid, perhaps even try and piece together a score. If you're playing at a decent lick, why should you have to keep moving over to let the golfing Schumachers past? Golf is not a sprint, and the only people who really benefit from being called through are those waved on. For everyone else, things only back up even more.

Part of the problem is that in an era where supply has outstripped demand, many private clubs have had to begrudgingly prise open their once firmly closed doors. Members who basked in exclusivity are increasingly having to co-exist with visitors to balance the club's books. The hounding is a tactical, well-planned response to ward off the unwelcome intruders so that they never return and normal service can be resumed. But these relics need to remember the only reason the visitors are there is because their club needs the money.

All golfers need to have mutual respect rather than mistrust for each other, whether by maintaining a sensible playing pace, or not constantly haranguing others. Those golfing hares who derive pleasure from hurtling round just so they can stand there, hands on hips, tutting, need to get a grip, get a life, get off a course on which others are trying to play a proper round at a reasonable pace, and go bunt their ball around some other piece of grass where they won't be irritating the hell out of others!

6
MENTAL GAME vs PHYSICAL GAME

Which is more crucial to success – the ability to think your way logically and sensibly round the course, staying in complete mental control of all the decisions you face, or possession of a swing that will stand the test physically when the heat is on, allowing you to play consistently and comfortably to your handicap most weeks?

MENTAL GAME

Estimates of the importance of golf's mental side relative to its physical one range from 10 per cent or less, to as much as 90 per cent from those a little more savvy. It certainly lies closer to the upper end of this scale than many golfers appreciate because we all have idiosyncrasies in our swings that are well enough ingrained to render physical change very hard without much more effort than we can realistically commit to.

Where we can more easily achieve progress is in our on-course thinking. A radical shift in philosophy is within everyone's grasp – if only they put their minds to it. Do you know someone who allows the outcome of one bad or unlucky shot to adversely affect several more – maybe even the rest of the round? Probably. What if that same golfer were to develop the ability to confine each miscue to the dustbin of the past and focus 100 per cent on the next shot? For one thing in golf is certain – once it's done it can't be undone. All you can ever do is influence what happens next, and a positive outcome is more likely if your mental state isn't flitting from the morose 'why does this always happen to me?' to out-and-out, blood-boiling rage.

For those who think of psychology as being mumbo-jumbo for the emotionally weak, what if we were to call it something else? Common sense, perhaps. How many shots do you sacrifice every round when you simply stop thinking straight?

We've all attempted shots we've got no idea how to play and have never practised, in some vain but futile bid to salvage bad situations. How many times have you tried to clear water that's right on your distance limit, or punch your ball through an unfeasible sliver of daylight in otherwise dense jungle? And how often have those irrational decisions backfired hideously, resulting in the big numbers you'd been so desperate to avoid? Why didn't you just lay up, knock it on, make bogey – maybe even save par – and keep that demoralising 'fat lady' off the scorecard? That way you'd be walking to the next tee eager to try again, rather than slipping into the kind of soul-destroying red mist that represents a one-way ticket to scorecard oblivion and a black mood for the rest of the day or even week.

Monty has gone on record as saying he could knock shots off the scores of average golfers if he were to caddy for them, simply by forcing them to play within, rather than beyond, their physical limits. He's absolutely spot on.

And if you're still not convinced of the mental game's importance, ask yourself this – why are those who pooh-pooh it the most the same ones you hear wittering on about pressure and confidence? Your muscles and body feel neither of these two sensations. They originate in your mind, which then processes them and sends out the messages that dictate physical performance. If your mind can filter out the worst negative vibes before they reach your muscles, you have a better chance of playing well. The mental and physical games are inextricably interlinked, but it is the former that is the controlling mechanism for every swing that follows.

PHYSICAL GAME

Golf is a sport requiring both physical and mental excellence. It would be obtuse to claim the irrelevance of the mental side of the game in comparison to the physical. Both attributes are crucial to success. What can, however, be argued is that the physical aspects are more fun. Booming drives, audacious shots over water, incredible escapes from seemingly hopeless positions – these are the shots that make the game entertaining and exciting. Not the strategic lay-up or the sensible lag putt. If you could perfect one of the two qualities being debated here, the physical game would have to get your vote.

The most exciting players to watch are always great exponents of the physical side of the game. John Daly tends to draw bigger crowds than Fred Funk, for instance. That's because Daly, with his huge power and immense physical talent, is enthralling to watch. You never know quite what you're going to get. He might make an incredible eagle by driving the green of a 350-yard par 4, flying a pond en route. Or he might find the pond, go in up to his ankles and try and blast it out. One thing's certain – he will attempt the carry. Funk on the other hand, although a great competitor, is a very short hitter. He finds fairways and plots his way effectively round each course he plays. But it's never edge-of-the-seat stuff.

There are times on a golf course when even the most clinical tactician has run out of options and only physical prowess can rectify the problem. A strategic brain will not help you escape knee-high rough. Careful course management will be of no assistance when 75-foot pine trees stand between you and the green and only a huge lofted sand wedge will get over. The importance of the physical game is evidenced by how much gym and cardiovascular work today's professionals do. Tiger Woods is an incredible physical specimen. Superfit, supple and strong, there are no circumstances on a golf course where he's prevented from doing something because of his physical limitations. If it's possible to cut the corner of a dog-leg, Tiger has the option to do it. If a par 5 is even vaguely reachable in two, he can get there.

Physical ability gives you a massive advantage over opponents. If you're outdriving them by 40 yards, not only will you be hitting shorter clubs into the green but you'll also be wearing them down psychologically. You can gain the upper hand mentally by dominating physically. The golf swing is a physically complicated act. To attain perfection you must be co-ordinated with great timing, flexibility and strength. Without a competent swing even the most mentally sharp will be unable to progress beyond a certain level. What would you rather be able to do – think a good game or actually play one?

7

CLUB MEMBERSHIP vs
PAY AND PLAY

In days gone by it was inconceivable that a keen golfer wouldn't be a member of a golf club. But due to the hectic and transient nature of many people's working lives, there are an increasing number of itinerant golfers who shun membership in favour of the country's numerous pay and play facilities. Who is getting the better experience?

CLUB MEMBERSHIP

The Saturday medal is reason enough for members' courses reigning supreme over the lowly pay and play. For the average amateur, club events are the staple of their competitive game. Trying to make the buffer zone, hoping for a top-ten finish in the Summer Cup to qualify for the Fitzherbert knockout, looking for a good showing in the President's Putter. There's nothing like it. It gives you something to play for, to strive towards and improve on. Touring around mediocre courses with little or no competitive objective, your game will not improve and you'll feel dissatisfied and unfulfilled.

There are many other compelling reasons to be a member of a club. You can meet new people (and they'll be golfers), get the expert advice and enjoy the banter of the club pro and take friends who are visiting down for a pint or a game of snooker. In many towns the golf club is a social hub. It's great to be a part of it.

It's fun perfecting how to negotiate your home track. You will learn its nuances and subtleties and when friends come to play they don't stand a chance as you know every break on every green and where all the trouble lies. On the flip side, just because you're a member of one club doesn't mean you can't tour around other venues. You can play in Opens with the handicap your club has given you, play club matches at other courses or make use of reciprocal discounts your club may have.

It used to be the case that members' clubs didn't welcome itinerant golfers. You could get on as a member's guest but not on spec. Those days are gone. There are very few clubs left in the UK that categorically refuse to accept visitors. There's also been a change in the mindset of the average member. They've begun to recognise the importance of accepting green fees in order to keep their annual subs down. They'll welcome you with open arms. If, for whatever reason, it's not appropriate or financially viable for you to join a club you can still play members' courses up and down the country for the price of a green fee.

Can you think of a pay and play course that exudes character and charm? No. They tend to be utilitarian and functional golf facilities. You turn up, hand over the money, play your five-hour round and leave. The experience of being a member is fun, rewarding and will stay with you for life. The best and friendliest examples will have you taking every opportunity to visit. Sitting in a comfortable old-style lounge in a studded leather armchair, sipping on the club drink, perusing the honours boards while one of the older members regales you with a tale about the time a badger stole Henry Longhurst's ball – that's a potential post-round scenario at a members' club. At the average pay and play you'll go into a building resembling a community centre, help yourself to a Cup-a-Soup from the vending machine and sit down on the plastic chairs they'd bought on the cheap from a local school. Not exactly inspiring.

PAY AND PLAY

The whole dynamic between pay and play courses and members' clubs has changed dramatically over the last 20 years. Back then the pay-and-player might have had a couple of courses to choose from in a 20-mile radius. Every other week he would head off to them in turn, flitting past scores of members' clubs on the way, whose gates remained firmly closed to him but whose fairways were becoming increasingly empty in many cases.

Everything has now changed on two counts. First, there are more pay and play facilities full stop. And second, a whole host of formerly unwelcoming members' clubs have been forced to open their doors for commercial reasons – and sometimes their very survival – often even participating in two-for-one and other dis-counted green fee schemes.

The course-building boom of the 1980s is largely responsible, leaving us with more courses but not the accompanying rise in participation levels needed to fill them. So the choice for the roving pay and play golfer has never been greater – or cheaper – to such an extent that many more of us are opting for this nomadic golfing existence in preference to the rigid confines of club membership.

Even if you're in an area of the country where subscriptions are more reasonably priced, do you really want to play the same course week in, week out? Perhaps it's no surprise that many one-time club members have even relinquished their memberships in favour of this more varied approach. And our ever busier lifestyles mean that often all we're looking for is to turn up somewhere, pay a reasonable green fee, play, perhaps have a quick drink and then get home to spend time with the kids or finish decorating the kitchen. No-strings-attached golf.

What fewer of us want is to spend good money joining a club which we then won't play at often enough to justify the subs. There'll be petty rules and regulations to contend with, politics will be rife and at some clubs you may even have to wear a jacket and tie just to sit in the clubhouse afterwards (while your wife sits outside!). On top of that, you may have to stump up for increased fees every now and then in respect of improvements that you neither believe in, nor will ever take advantage of, simply because the consensus vote carried the proposals through.

So why not simply pay for what you really want – a round of not-too-expensive golf at a different course to the one you played last week. OK, some pay and play facilities are overused, overcrowded goat tracks that take 5 hours to get round and are probably ankle-deep in mud through the winter. But many these days are not. And with all those revenue-seeking members' clubs also now at your beck and call for relatively little cost, think of the fun you could have ticking off a different course every week – in many cases paying less per round than the average member does at those clubs.

Yes, itinerant golf is the way ahead, winning hands down for variety, cost and, perhaps most importantly of all, freedom from the straitjacket of club membership.

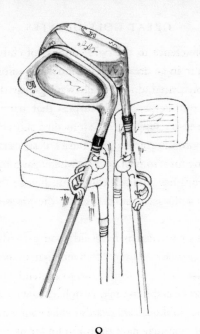

8

BLADES vs CAVITY BACKS

Play well with blades and the feeling is hard to beat; play poorly and you may never want to step on a golf course again. Cavity-back irons forgive all but the most heinous of strikes and allow higher handicappers to hit the ball further and straighter more frequently. The question is, are they a cop-out?

BLADES

What is more satisfying, completing *The Times* 'fiendish' sudoku puzzle or completing the *TV Quick* super-easy, only-two-numbers-missing sudoku puzzle? Yes, the former. Now translate that thought process to golf. Which is preferable, playing to handicap using a sleek and stylish set of classic blades, or playing to handicap with a chunky set of cumbersome and unattractive cavity backs? The former may be a more difficult proposition, but when achieved it's infinitely more rewarding.

There's no point in arguing that blades are easier to use than cavity backs, because they're not. If you're a beginner then blades are not for you. Blades are something you should aspire to as your golf improves: a sort of coming-of-age golfing graduation. It's like removing the stabilisers from your bike. With cavity backs you have a safety net but no kudos and less excitement. With blades you've become a man, people want to be your friend and you feel like a hero.

People argue that golf is about enjoyment and that cavity-back clubs allow you to enjoy the game more. But playing a great shot with a classic blade delivers a huge amount of unparalleled enjoyment. When a bladed club is struck sweetly the feeling is incredible. The ball zips off the clubface and you're left with an untouchable sensation that you've just achieved something special. Even the cleanest hits with a cavity back don't feel that good. The dull thud of impact doesn't set the pulse racing or the adrenalin flowing.

When you master how to use a set of blades the number of shot options open to you increases greatly. You find you can actually shape the ball and really feel the shot. It's difficult to get any feel from a cavity back the size of a waffle toaster. The ball flight produced by a blade is penetrating and powerful; a cavity back will generate a high wafting shot that gets buffeted by even the slightest breeze. The cavity back is also prone to produce the 'rogue flier': one that comes right out of the middle and, for some inexplicable reason, travels 20 yards further than you're normally able to hit it. You tend to produce this shot when out of bounds lies behind a green. You don't get that with blades, they're far more consistent.

How good gleaming blades look in the bag. They suggest their owner is a 'player' – someone you wouldn't want to face in the club knockout. By contrast, cavity-back clubs are uncommonly ugly and inspire revulsion rather than respect. How can you maintain any level of pride when you've got a bag full of sticks that look more like workmen's tools than golf clubs? You'll love and cherish a set of blades, polish them and keep the grooves clear. You'll be reluctant to leave them, unlike cavity backs that you'll probably change more often than a baby's nappy. You'll keep your beloved blades in your bedroom and occasionally go across the room to stroke them or read them a bedtime story.

CAVITY BACKS

Pure blades are golf's hellfire and damnation preachers, condemning you to disproportionate punishment for even the tiniest of ball-striking sins. On the other hand, cavity-back irons are the game's great high priests, absolving you from a wide variety of mishit transgressions and granting you rewards you perhaps don't really deserve. This is precisely why they're far and away the best option for golfers for whom the centre of the clubface might as well be a distant planet on a galaxy far, far away – which is about 99 per cent of people who play the game.

Oh yes, it's true that visually, blades are mighty alluring. They hold a siren-like fascination for many with their sleek lines and high-lustre finishes. But don't be drawn in. They're only trying to lure you on to the rocks – or at least into the trees and bushes. Just as they are cursed with tiny heads, uniform weight distribution and edges you can almost cut yourself on, so cavity backs are blessed with oversized heads, added weight around the perimeters where you most need it, and edges so nicely rounded you could leave a tiny baby playing with them quite safely.

The end result is forgiveness on a scale blades just can't comprehend. So when you make contact off-centre, out of the toe or too close to the bottom of the club, you'll enjoy far greater distance and accuracy than your strike really warrants. Don't we all need some of that? A word of warning, though – they are performance enhancers, not miracle workers, and your very worst strikes will still get exactly the results they deserve.

The benefits of cavity backs are similar to those enjoyed by tennis and squash players when their racquets evolved from heavy wooden affairs to light graphite ones, allowing a quantum leap in head size. The modern squash racquet has grown to roughly the size of the old wooden tennis ones, which makes it all the more perplexing that when Björn Borg chose to launch an ill-advised comeback in the early 1990s he did so brandishing his old wooden racquet. And less surprising that he kept getting hammered in the first round by complete nobodies armed with state-of-the-art modern ones. The game had moved on to such an extent that it's just possible that Venus Williams armed with a modern racquet would beat the John McEnroe of yesteryear wielding his wooden one. But that's mere speculation.

What is not mere speculation is that golf irons have also moved on in the same way. So you can either stay stuck in the past, deluding yourself that the feedback you get from a shot sent careering into the trees with a blade is of more value than one off the toe with a cavity back that still scrapes on to the fringe, or you can get with the times. Seems a straightforward choice, really.

9

GOLF ABROAD vs
GOLF AT HOME

*The itinerant British golfer is spoilt for choice. Right on the doorstep
there's an incredible selection of the world's best courses – links, heath
and parkland. But can those layouts beat playing in foreign climes over
immaculately maintained courses with the sun on your back?*

GOLF ABROAD

It would be churlish to suggest that golf at home isn't enjoyable, but
there are clearly sound supply and demand reasons as to why the
southern Spanish coast, for example, is now one continuous lush
golf course interspersed with hotels, villas and ever-present cranes to
create yet more of the same.

Weather is the key consideration here, and although you can occasionally get caught out in Spain, Portugal, Florida or any other sunny oasis, the chances are slim compared to those in good old Blighty. Even if you do, you know the sun's warming rays will soon be back out to dry you off and have you bouncing jauntily along the fairways once more in a 'does life get any better than this?' manner. Back home, you'd still be trudging round with your head sunk Montyesque into your shoulders, wondering just what you're doing out there on such a godforsaken day.

Just a couple of days' golf in the sun gives your skin the kind of healthy glow that prompts people to seriously underestimate your age. After several sunless outings in the UK, your pallid, dulled complexion is more likely to have people discussing the likelihood of you seeing the year out!

Golf in the sun has an unrushed feel about it too. Yes, it may take a little longer than normal if you get stuck behind a four-ball of novice Continental hackers. But where the heckles would be rising back home, somehow it doesn't seem to matter in the sun. You dilly and dally, chatting away with your playing partners and maybe even tarrying a while at the halfway hut to enjoy the odd sangria or two. If you're lucky, there's even a chance of nipping past them in your buggy, while they spend the obligatory 15 minutes searching for Helga's ball in the barren scrub 50 yards from the tee. There's a real sense of jingoistic achievement in that.

The weather conditions that you're so enjoying are equally beneficial to the golf courses too. They're invariably in far better condition for more of the year than those in Britain – a real pull for anyone whose home club begins to resemble the Somme after days on end of winter wetness. And wouldn't you rather be putting on greens of finest silk than cheap acrylic shag pile?

While those Continental novices may not always be particularly good at the game itself, they win hands down in the fashion stakes, bringing an unprecedented sense of style to the fairways. It's easy to spot the Brits abroad – him in a thick cotton polo, beige slacks and unnecessarily heavyweight golf shoes, her in an outfit with a hint of the schoolmarm or librarian about it.

Meanwhile our European cousins have discovered colour and flattering fits in a big way and are not ashamed to flaunt it – whether male or female. If you strike lucky, you may even stumble across the Italians with the voluptuous daughter who sees no reason not to wear the same tight-fitting, flesh-revealing clothes on the course as she would off it – and neither do you! The lady captain back home would be apoplectic with rage – or is that jealousy? – but seeing *her* in a figure-hugging outfit showing a bit of leg would be enough to put you right off your game, wouldn't it?

GOLF AT HOME

Wherever you live in the UK, stop a moment and count the number of golf courses within a 50-mile radius of your front door. It will probably take you some time. There are over 2,500 golf courses in Britain, approximately one-tenth of all the courses worldwide. When you consider that Britain makes up just 0.05 per cent of the world's surface, it's a pretty impressive concentration.

Because Britain is so compact all of our courses are wonderfully accessible. If you live in London you can reach northerly golfing outposts like Dornoch and Nairn via a one-hour-15-minute flight to Inverness and a short drive. A few days playing those fantastic and historic layouts will leave an indelible imprint on the memory; it'll also be affordable and convenient. It's difficult to understand why anyone would overlook that option and endure an expensive nine-hour flight to somewhere like Orlando to go and play soulless, monotonous, utilitarian layouts. The weather might be better but that's about it.

Britain's golfers can become blinkered. There's a great culture of 'the grass is greener' at golf clubs up and down the country: 'Oh, you should see the courses on the Costa del Sol.' Or: 'We played some magnificent layouts in Phuket.' Very good, but you could have saved yourself a long journey and travelled to somewhere equally good, if not better, far closer to home.

Lest we forget the embarrassment of fantastic golf courses sitting right on our doorstep, here's a reminder.

Golf began on the linksland of eastern Scotland. Around our magnificent coastline there exists the most incredible collection of rugged seaside courses anywhere in the world. We have the Home of Golf at St Andrews. 'The Auld Grey Toon' is a Mecca for golfing tourists across the globe. St Andrews is an incredible place crammed with history, myth and misty-eyed memories. Also on the coast we have the other Open venues; there are 14 of them in total. We can go to any of these courses for a game and tread in the footsteps of the sport's paladins almost any day of almost any week.

Links is golf in its purest form. Courses in other countries attempt imitation but why accept second best? From Royal Aberdeen to Royal Troon, Royal County Down to St Enodoc and Royal Birkdale to Royal St George's, Britain is blessed with the most incredible links in the world.

In England's 'green and pleasant land' we have some of the most interesting and picturesque inland courses on earth. Old layouts like Walton Heath, Sunningdale and Wentworth have been joined by superb modern developments such as the Grove and Bearwood Lakes.

So next time you're considering a golfing trip, think hard: travel within our country, saving time and money to play the world's best courses, or spend a small fortune and waste hours in planes and airports to go and play courses that are desperately trying to replicate what's already on offer in Britain. It's a pretty straightforward choice.

10

PRO SHOP vs
HIGH STREET STORE

The golfing public has never had so many options when it comes to buying golf equipment. The traditional club pro shop is coming under increasing pressure from large high street retailers selling top-of-the-range brands at super-low prices. The question is, does the pro shop still have something to offer?

PRO SHOP

It's an undeniable and sad fact of our consumer-driven society that club pros can no longer match the prices on offer at the well-known high street retailers. But what the pro shop continues to offer is far more valuable than a low price tag. Buy from the pro and you gain the benefit of his experience and expertise.

Imagine you're in the market for a new 3-wood. Which of the following options sounds more appealing?

(a) You visit your friendly club pro. He knows you and your game well. He knows the standard you play to and your likely budget. You chat through some of the options and he selects a few models for you to try. He tapes them up and accompanies you to the practice ground to watch you hit balls. He carefully assesses your performance with each of the clubs and gives his honest opinion on the merits or short-comings of each. You come to a mutual decision on the 3-wood that's right for you and you purchase it, entirely satisfied you've made an informed and accurate decision. A year later you are still using the club and are playing well with it.

(b) You see an advert on a billboard that a nearby high street retailer is selling big brand fairway woods at 30 per cent off. You go through the automatic doors, wrestle past the throng of people hovering around the rack and pick one up. You look around for guidance but nobody is there to tell you about the club or what shaft you should opt for. You decide to bite the bullet and head for the till. A spotty adolescent swipes the bar code and holds out his hand for payment. Theoretically you seem to have secured a bargain, but when you get out on the course and realise you can't hit the club for toffee, the deal suddenly tastes a little less sweet.

The pro is vital to the infrastructure of his club and it's upsetting how often he's taken for granted by the members he serves. He must have excellent PR skills to deal with society visits and field complaints from tricky members; he must be firm but fair with the club's juniors; he must be a good manager, not just looking after his staff but often the start sheet as well. At many clubs the professional will also give advice on the set-up of the course, its condition or any proposed alterations.

It's grotesquely unfair when people use the professional's expertise with no intention of repaying him for it. An increasing number of people go to the pro shop for advice on a new piece of equipment, but on getting the required information go and buy the item elsewhere. If you want club pros to survive and continue to be a source of advice, you have to support them.

So take the pro's advice wherever possible, both on your game and your equipment. In return, give him your custom. You may be able to get a driver £15 cheaper at a high street shop but the slapdash staff there won't watch you swing it, confirm it's the right model for you and then take you for a beer in the clubhouse.

HIGH STREET STORE

High street golf stores are to pro shops as supermarkets are to humble corner shops – the inevitable face of progress in a capitalist world where buying power, and therefore price, are king, whether you like it or not.

'Terrible, just terrible,' people cry as their local shop closes its shutters for the final time, browbeaten and defeated. But these are the same people who load up the supermarket trolley to the hilt every week, only ever nipping round the corner for a tin of tomatoes or pint of milk when they get caught short.

And so it is with pro shops. We may still buy the odd club-crested sweater or sleeve of balls if we find the bag empty, but we snub them when it comes to serious purchases as the high street's inexorable double pull of choice and rock-bottom prices is too much to resist. And just as with the supermarkets, there's no turning back.

To be fair, part of the problem lies with manufacturers who are in a perpetual war with each other to bring new gear before an eager golfing public. Product cycles are far shorter than they used to be. The poor pro is often left holding full-price kit long after the manufacturer has decided to sell all remaining warehouse stock at a daft price to one of the high street chains. But where there are losers, so too are there winners, and in this particular scenario the winner is you, the customer, whose overriding concern nowadays is the size of the figure following the pound sign.

The high street is invariably cheaper anyway, but when it comes to these bargains, many of us would rather save tens, perhaps hundreds, of pounds than have the very latest kit, especially when performance gains are likely to be inversely disproportional to the sum saved.

Then there's the matter of confused business relationships, for while the high street transaction is a straight customer–retailer one, in the pro shop friendship may also be involved, with members often knowing the pro outside traditional transaction boundaries. The maxim 'never mix business with pleasure' was never truer, for while the member will inevitably be seeking the pleasure of a favourable deal, it will rarely be to the pro's business advantage. 'What can you do for me?' is a phrase the 21st-century pro hears every single day, and he invariably has to cut a deal if his name isn't to be mud around the clubhouse. Aggrieved members have very loud voices.

With their feet nailed to the floor and their margins almost extinct, it's little wonder many pros have virtually abandoned the shop, and sought to make up the lost revenue by begrudgingly reverting to the crowded teaching schedules they'd long since hoped to have left behind.

The average pro simply can't compete on price or choice and, much as we may occasionally feel the odd pang of guilt or compassion, business is business and we'd be fools to pay more for something than we really have to. Harsh, but fair.

11
WATCHING GOLF ON TV vs WATCHING LIVE

As a golf spectator, just where is the best place to follow the action – on a screen perched on your sideboard where you'll never miss a shot and enjoy all your home comforts, or actually live at the course where you can breathe in the whole tournament atmosphere and perhaps track your favourite player all the way round?

WATCHING ON TV

There are few experiences in the life of a keen golfer that are more exciting than the first time they travel to watch a live golf tournament. Having viewed the best pros on television, the prospect of seeing them in the flesh is a thrilling one.

But, after an exhausting eight hours of traipsing round a links, snatching the occasional glimpse of Ernie Els' hat or Darren Clarke's caddy, the excitement has dwindled somewhat. They feel they've barely seen any of the play and have absolutely no idea what's going on in the golf tournament.

It's a shame, but it's a fact – golf is better viewed from the comfort of your favourite armchair parked in front of the TV.

Watching the golf on the television you won't miss a second of the action. Every crucial putt that drops, every drive that's striped and every wayward shot that costs a competitor his chance of glory: you'll see them all. Better than that, you'll see them a couple of times, sometimes in slow motion. You'll see exactly why the ball ended in the bunker or get confirmation that the shot did, indeed, hit the flag.

Watching on TV you'll be constantly updated with the scoring. You'll find out instantaneously whether Tiger made his putt at the 12th to go five under. On top of this you'll be furnished with an incredible range of statistics revealing everything from which hole is playing the hardest to who is finding the most fairways. You'll also hear the experts' opinions on how the play is progressing. Ex-professionals and experienced journalists, who know the game and the players inside out, will share their thoughts and divulge the odd amusing anecdote about the sport, past and present.

There are more benefits to watching the golf at home: you don't have to face the nightmare of travelling to the tournament – terrible traffic jams and courtesy buses if you drive, the worry of the event going to a playoff and you missing your last train home if you opt for public transport – it happened at Carnoustie in 1999. It's also considerably cheaper watching from your sitting room. Tickets for this year's Open are £55 for the day. If you take the family you're looking at a pretty epic bill. Add: the cost of travel, a programme at £6.50, bacon rolls at £5 a pop, a couple of beers, some logo merchandise and you'll be straight on the phone to the Halifax to try and organise a second mortgage.

Most sports work when viewed live because you see almost all of the action. Sitting around a tennis court or football pitch you'll witness 99% of the play. Unfortunately, it just doesn't work with golf. Spend a day watching a golf tournament live and you'd be lucky to witness 1% of the play first hand. If you love the sport of golf there's only one winner when it comes to watching it – put the kettle on or crack open a beer and make yourself comfy.

WATCHING LIVE

There's no doubt it's convenient having pictures beamed into your living room covering all the key action with replays and expert analysis. But if watching golf there is like looking at a photo of a glorious view, then watching it live is like venturing out to experience that view for yourself in all its three-dimensional, multi-sensory splendour. The only senses you use watching on TV are sight and sound, with much of the latter obliterated by incessant commentary.

At the course there's no commentary and the sound is the real, unadulterated thing. Nothing compares to the echoing ring of a crisply struck iron as one of the world's best despatches a shot towards a distant target between rows of towering trees at Wentworth, or the roar of sea and wind as another attempts a tricky putt, trousers flapping furiously, at one of our great Open Championship links.

You'll use your sense of smell too to breathe in freshly cut grass, salty sea air, blooming flora or forest pine as you stroll round. The closest you'll get to that at home is an unconvincing replication of the latter two from your plug-in 'Room-o-fresh', which is only marginally preferable to the smells of wet dog and last night's Rogan

Josh you're so eager to conceal. Feel comes into play too. You can feel the earth move under your feet, sense any moisture in the air, feel for yourself how long or wiry the rough is and so on.

In other words, you get the full picture rather than the partial one even the Highest Definition TV can deliver. So you'll have a better understanding of the test the course poses on a given day than even the TV commentators, whose on-course experience is typically whatever they glimpse on the well-furrowed path from commentary box to Bollinger tent. There are no interruptions either – no commercial breaks and no sharing with coverage of the racing from Haydock. At The Open, you can watch from dawn to dusk – potentially 14 hours of viewing – which makes the £50 or so entrance fee seem a snip compared with a premier league football ticket.

And to those who say, 'but you miss out on all the vital action', try watching in a different way, as it makes a fascinating alternative to the standard TV fare. Follow one player from 1st tee to 18th green. See how one man's round really pans out – the highs and lows, the good breaks and bad breaks. Should that 71 really have been four shots better or five shots worse? Only you and the player will know exactly how it all added up to the final figure. Or try observing all the action from one point – perhaps a par-3 tee or green. See how different players tackle the tee shot or set about trying to save par.

This year then, rather than settling for the life of a goggle-eyed golf fan, put down the remote, step away from the set and head down to an actual event, whether it's The Open, a tour stop or even some local top level amateur stuff. You'll find it makes a refreshing change to use nearly all your senses as a golf spectator.

Sawgrass: the 17th.

12
PAR 3S vs
PAR 5S

What length hole really is king of the course – the one-shotter, where a satisfying, crisply struck iron could leave you minutes away from a share of the 'twos sweep', or the three-shotter, where the right blend of skill and power could represent your best chance of a rare birdie or, better still, the even rarer eagle?

PAR 3S

On what grounds can par 5s possibly be considered the stars of the golf course? At many well-established clubs they often measure less than 500 yards and are among the easiest and most uninspiring holes you'll play. All you have to do is nudge the ball forwards 160 yards three times and hey presto – a simple two-putt par at worst and, for the average handicapper, three points in a Stableford more often than not. With modern drivers and long-iron alternatives like utility clubs to hand, they're really little more than long par 4s for many golfers, who regularly make mincemeat out of them as a result. Par 5s are quite simply golf's great giveaway.

Not so the par 3 – the real star of the course for a host of reasons. They come in all shapes and sizes from under 100 yards to the very threshold of par 4 distance – uphill or downhill; playing across side slopes, valleys, lakes and sometimes even the sea; from the well protected to the apparently defenceless, boasting targets that range from large and inviting to virtually invisible.

Yet despite their thousand and one different guises, all ask one essential question of the golfer: do you have not only the vision and creativity required to pick the right club for the distance and conditions, but also the skill and nerve to execute the shot? On the best-designed par 3s, the scoring prospects generated by good or bad tee shots can be poles apart – strike it well and a birdie putt awaits; miss it in the wrong place and you can kiss goodbye to not only par, but bogey as well.

Chances are if you're looking at a club's website or brochure you'll find reference to a 'signature hole' and a princely sum says that in the vast majority of instances, that signature hole will be a par 3 – either for its sheer photogenic beauty or cunning complexity of design. At Augusta, for example, the short but treacherous 12th – the Golden Bell – has often rung the death knell for someone's Masters challenge; at Royal Troon the world-famous Postage Stamp represents perhaps the most hazardous 123 yards in major championship golf; and at Sawgrass, the island green 17th needs no introduction to even the most infrequent PGA Tour watcher – or the host of top names who have sent many a ball to a watery grave there over the years. Name one par 5 that conjures up such instant widespread recognition.

To close the case for par 3s, just remember that in every round you play they offer up a handful of chances to achieve golf's ultimate glory shot – the hole-in-one. OK, albatrosses (three under par on one hole) may be rarer beasts, but they are only really within the grasp of proficient players capable of hitting the ball decent distances. Anyone, on the other hand, can have a hole-in-one, as evidenced by regular local paper sports page reports of 5-year-olds and 90-year-olds who have achieved just such a feat. And how many clubs do you know that have an albatross honours board hanging proudly in the bar?

PAR 5S

A par 5 is like an elegant, long-legged beauty queen. Stretching enticingly into the distance, she tempts you to win her favour. To do it you must have mastery over every element of your game. You must have worked out a clear strategy and be completely confident. A par 3 is the dumpy librarian of golf holes – neither enticing nor seductive. If you can be bothered to try and win her favour you won't have to work too hard. Just play one decent iron shot.

Par 5s are by far the best holes on a golf course because they represent a complete test of golf:

- *Driving* – straight, consistent driving is essential. Even if you don't expect to get up in two, it's crucial you get yourself in play well down the fairway.
- *Long game* – players who can hit the ball a good distance can enjoy this advantage on a par 5. They might be able to reach the green in two and set up the chance of a thrilling eagle. Even if the green is too distant it's important to play a solid second

shot ending in the correct position from where to approach the green.

- *Short game* – if you go for the green you'll miss it more often than not. For this reason your short game has to be sharp to afford the best chance of getting up and down. If you've chosen to lay up you must be a good pitcher to try and set up a birdie chance.

- *Strategy* – where should you position your tee shot? Should you go for the green over the water? Where should you lay up? Which is the best side to miss on if you don't find the green? Course management is a key element of golf and it comes to the fore on par 5s.

- *Recovery* – a par 5 allows for swashbuckling, Seve-style golf. If you've driven poorly into the trees you can still chip out sideways, play a third down towards the green and make par or even birdie. On a par 3, one bad shot will generally lead to bogey or worse – all a bit hit and miss really.

In professional events the par 5 always offers an exciting opportunity for a competitor who's off the pace. The long hole can generate massive swings in fortune. The leader makes a bogey while his nearest challenger fires in a fantastic eagle; suddenly there's a new name atop the leaderboard.

Let's take a course we all know as an example – Augusta. Yes, the par 3 12th is a fabulous hole, but it's totally eclipsed by the par 5s that follow. The 13th and 15th both offer the purest examples of risk and reward. It's on these holes The Masters is won and lost.

Consider this finally. Is it preferable for a course to end with a par 3 or par 5? If you can honestly say you like a course to finish with a par 3 then you're a lost cause.

Phil Mickelson   Miguel Angel Jimenez

13
EUROPEAN TOUR vs
PGA TOUR

The two premier men's golf tours are constantly competing to attract the biggest names in the game. The PGA Tour offers huge purses and more world-ranking points while the European Tour offers pros the chance to compete all over the world on some amazingly diverse courses. Which circuit has the edge?

EUROPEAN TOUR

The European Tour is an international extravaganza travelling to 25 countries around the globe. It features charismatic players from five continents testing themselves in differing climates over varying courses throughout the season. Compare it to the PGA Tour – an insular money-driven weekly putting competition between one-dimensional characterless clones over one-dimensional characterless courses. There's simply no comparison. The European Tour is in a different class.

Let's start with what the PGA Tour has to offer. Primarily, it's money. With the introduction of the FedEx Cup, total prize money on the 2008 PGA Tour was over $250 million. Very impressive, but why should we care how much richer Tiger Woods is going to be? The PGA Tour is dragging golf to the edge of the abyss. We've watched football lose itself in a corporate whirl since the inception of the English Premiership. Teams have become corporations and overpaid players commodities to be traded. As a result the game has lost its passion. If Tim Finchem and his cronies at the PGA Tour have their way, golf will go down the same road. It already has the directions.

Watching coverage of the PGA Tour is torturous. First, it's infuriating how everything is sponsored: 'OK, Bobby, let's have a look at the line of that putt on the Telestrator. It's sponsored by McDermott's Diarrhea Tablets. They stem the flow in just 5 minutes.' Then there's the crowd. It's difficult to bear it when someone cries out 'Get in the goddamn hole!' as Chaz Hoffermaier plays out of a bunker backwards. Let's not even start on the courses they play. 'Hi there, welcome to coverage of the Greater Missouri Classic from the Little Urchin Course at Majestic Moon River Country Club.' Appalling. All the courses look the same – wide curving fairways flanked by enormous flat white bunkers and dyed-blue ponds leading to huge manicured greens. You'll see a lot of these greens as it's here the tournaments are decided. All the faceless nobodies plodding round with their caps hiding their faces can smack it miles and fly high approaches into these massive receptive targets. It means only putting can separate them. 'Here's Brent

Scudamaker from 68 feet. And he's got another one.' It's monotonous and boring.

No two weeks are the same on the European Tour. It's anything but boring. From courses forged out of the Arabian desert to the windswept links of Carnoustie, from the mountains of Switzerland to the South African plains – each tournament delivers a unique challenge and requires the mastery of different skills. Here lies a key reason for the European Tour's superiority – the versatility and adaptability of the players. They're thrown into a different set of circumstances each week and must learn to cope with them. It's a principal reason for the European superiority over the Yanks when it comes to the Ryder Cup this century. Boo Weekley might play well over the repetitive stadium courses on the PGA Tour, but show him a windswept Birkdale and he misses the cut comfortably.

There may not be as much money up for grabs on the European Tour, but this is more than made up for by the quality of the venues and the ability of the players who battle it out in captivating and enthralling competitions week after week.

PGA TOUR

Like it or not, America's PGA Tour eclipses the European Tour on so many counts that, to all intents and purposes, it is now golf's World Tour. America hosts three of golf's four majors, looks set to hog the World Golf Championship events for the foreseeable future and boasts golf's unofficial fifth major – the Players' Championship – which regularly attracts one of the strongest fields of the season.

Prize funds are vastly superior, as are course conditions and the facilities for the players. Crowds are huge too. In the more obscure European Tour outposts there can be more people inside the ropes than out. And unfortunately, towards the end of an era in which the exploits of Europe's big six – Ballesteros, Faldo, Lyle, Woosnam, Langer and Olazábal – had taken the European Tour to the very brink of the PGA Tour for status and wealth, along came a certain Mr Woods attracting dollars like they were going out of fashion and sending PGA Tour prize funds spiralling way beyond those in Europe.

In 2008 the lowest purse on the PGA Tour was $3 million, with the winner's share a not-to-be-sniffed-at $540,000; in Europe, David Dixon pocketed just €100,000 for winning the Saint-Omer Open. Most first prizes in America nudge, and often pass, the $1 million barrier. Whether or not that's obscene for four days' work is another debate – but it's certainly one of the main reasons several Europeans have now made the States their permanent base, and why many more are plying their trade there with ever-greater frequency. Who can blame them? For such are the riches on offer that to keep your card on the PGA Tour last year you needed to earn a not insubstantial $853,000; on the European Tour it was a paltry €230,000.

Looking at the world ranking, at the time of writing 63 of the top 100 were PGA Tour regulars while only 30 played in Europe, many of whom split their schedules across both tours. No Americans come and play in Europe unless a big sweetener is on offer, perhaps some time around The Open when they have to cross the pond anyway. It really is one-way traffic across the Atlantic.

If all that wasn't enough, the fact that PGA Tour events take place in a time zone more amenable to European golf watchers rubs further salt into the wound. The European Tour happens while we're all grafting away for a living; the PGA Tour is beamed into our living rooms when we've got home from work, packed the kids off to bed and are ready to relax for a couple of hours. Perfect.

A simple analogy to round things off – if the PGA Tour were football's Premier League then the European Tour would be its

Championship. People watch and follow the former two simply because they're where the best players or teams are playing. Watching Tiger, Phil and Vijay slug it out is a bit like watching Chelsea take on Manchester United. But apart from a few diehards, who really wants to watch Doncaster take on Barnsley or Alejandro Cañizares go head to head with David Drysdale in the Russian Open?

Colin Montgomerie -
reliable fade

14
FADE vs
DRAW

Although the objective of most golfers is to hit the ball straight, everybody tends to shape the ball either left to right (a fade) or right to left (a draw). Both shot shapes have their advantages, but both also have some fairly significant drawbacks in their most extreme forms: think slice and hook.

FADE

The choice between fade and draw is equally one between control and distance, courtesy of the different types of spin the two shots generate. As Lee Trevino once famously said, 'You can talk to a fade but a hook won't listen!' OK, a hook may be an exaggerated draw, but the sentiment remains the same.

Of course, you only have to mention the word 'distance' for something to go straight to the top of most golfers' wish lists. The only things that generate clubhouse bragging rights are sadly either how far you hit it or how little club you hit into such and such a green – both of which a draw can help. But is the draw really all it's cracked up to be?

If we look to tennis for a comparison, the fade would be the drop shot, landing like the proverbial butterfly with sore feet and leaving your opponent lunging desperately for the ball at full stretch; the draw would be the powerful topspin drive, outpacing your opponent's reactions and sending the ball whizzing past him cross court or down the line. In tennis, both shots are of equal merit. In golf the draw can be as dangerously uncontrollable as the fade is safe and predictable.

A ball that hits the fairway with draw spin pitches with unnecessary venom, sending your ball onwards and leftwards into potential trouble off the fairway; fade spin will see your ball dropping softly back to earth, staying close to where it lands and leaving you in prime position to attack. Yes, with a fade you'll probably be looking ahead to see where your opponent is, but the sight that greets your eye will often be of him scrabbling around in thorny bushes, fraying both precious lambswool sweater and temper while frantically seeking a way back into play without a penalty drop.

It's the same story into the greens, where a controlled fade will land, stop and maybe even spin back a little from its higher flight. The lower-flying draw will react like a cat on a hot tin roof at midday in Cairo, scampering on towards the trouble at the back and placing mounting pressure on your scrambling skills.

The draw does have distance going for it, but that's about it.

Playing with a draw will leave you constantly close to the edge, increasing the need for precision just to keep the thing on the course. The fade allows greater margin for error, as even if you're a little off-line, you know your ball won't be going far when it lands.

To conclude the case for the fade, there are two very good reasons not to be remotely concerned about the distance you're sacrificing. First, most traditional UK courses have been overtaken to a certain degree by equipment technology, so distance is rarely as pressing a requirement as accuracy. And secondly, take a long hard look at Colin Montgomerie's record of seven straight European Order of Merit titles – and eight in total. All were won with a game built around a reliable fade, helping him hit fairways and greens for fun – as sound a commendation as you could ever want.

DRAW

Let's get straight to the point. How many of us wish we could hit a consistent draw? For most amateurs the draw is a golfing Holy Grail. It's a mysterious skill beyond our ken, the preserve of the professional or the elite amateur. The great golfing teacher and philosopher Harvey Penick said: 'If you hit a slice you are not going to get any better as a player.' A fade is just a slice waiting to happen. The draw is a powerful, aggressive shot. It's an impressive sight and one that will have onlookers making comments like 'What a lovely shape' or 'This boy can play a bit.' The fade is a feeble excuse for a golf shot and will have onlookers making comments like 'Just leaked a touch' or 'Shame about the wee tail on it.'

Most club players want to be able to hit the ball further. They spend huge sums of money on the latest driver or super-distance ball. But they're not investing their money wisely. They could add 30 yards to each drive by taking some lessons to learn how to hit a draw. By moving the ball right to left, topspin will be imparted on it.

When it hits the ground it'll kick on like a hungry cheetah that's just spotted a dozy antelope. In the summer months you'll get huge amounts of run, and drive the ball incredible distances as a result. With a fade, backspin is imparted on the ball, causing a dramatic loss in distance. The ball will fly higher and the backspin will mean that it stops quickly on landing.

Into the wind the fade is a simply hopeless shot. The left-to-right movement will be exaggerated and the backspin will cause the shot to balloon. The ball will be coming backwards by the time it hits the ground. The slight draw will bore through the wind like a hot knife through butter. The man who plays a draw is at a distinct advantage when the breeze is against.

Go to the practice ground at any professional tournament and you'll witness a row of the game's greatest exponents shaping the ball from right to left. OK, there are exceptions like Monty, but the vast majority of top professionals play their shots with a slight draw. Why is this? Simple, it's already been said. The draw is a superior shot; it goes further, the flight is more penetrating and it's easier to control.

In the hands of a top pro the fade can be a useful shot. They can make the ball fly high and land softly on hard greens. For the average golfer, however, the fade is far from desirable. A high floater drifting short and right is not a strong shot. The low chasing draw is preferable in every way.

15
STROKE PLAY vs MATCH PLAY

In stroke play it's just you against the course, nobody else can affect the result. In match play it's a man-on-man contest – the single objective is to defeat your opponent or opponents. But which format makes for a more interesting and appropriate test of your golfing ability?

STROKE PLAY

A possible match play scenario – it's the latter stages of a club knockout competition and you're on sparkling form. Your opponent in the quarter-finals is Chopper Macpherson, a 26 handicapper who's never finished in the top ten of a monthly medal. Quite rightly you feel quietly confident.

Hole one and Chopper tees off first. He hooks it out of bounds. You leisurely play one down the middle. He then tops his third off the tee, slices another out of bounds, fats two shots then thins one through the back. Meanwhile, you've caressed a shot to 3 feet for an almost certain birdie. After a double hit behind the green Chopper picks up – he would have recorded about a 14. You're one up. The next is a par 3 where you play one nicely to the heart of the green. Chopper slices one wildly, it strikes a tree and pings back just short of the putting surface. He then knifes a chip that strikes the flag at about 15 miles per hour. Unbelievably it drops into the cup – back to all-square. You continue to play solidly all round, well under handicap. Chopper's score is closer to 200 than 100 but, owing to his ridiculous inconsistency and brazen good fortune, the match is all-square at the last where he's getting two shots. For the first time in the game he plays the hole reasonably and records a regulation par. You would need an eagle for the half but your second shot lips out and you lose the match. Match play is an unfair test of golf and an unrealistic representation of the game.

Stroke play is true golf because it always identifies the golfer who has played best on any given day. In order to win a stroke play competition you must perform consistently well over 18 holes. There's no better feeling than returning to the clubhouse having compiled a great score. Your post-round pint will taste sweet. Does it go down so well after you've scraped a match play victory in a low-standard contest you didn't really deserve to win?

If match play were superior then the majority of professional events would be played to that format. They're not. Can you imagine The Open as a match play tournament? Tiger Woods has a bit of a ropey round on day one and gets knocked out by an on-form Santiago Luna, Robert Rock plays a blinder and knocks out Ernie Els, while Sergio loses on the first extra hole to Robert-Jan Derksen. Sunday afternoon sees a less than thrilling final between Bretts

Rumford and Wetterich – it doesn't sound very appealing, does it? Four-round stroke play gives players a chance to have a poor spell and recover. The best man will always win. Yes, the few match play tournaments held through the season are entertaining, but they're a novelty and often throw up disappointing results.

Stroke play will continue to be the preferred format as long as the sport of golf exists. When chatting to a colleague or friend about the game they're very likely to ask you what your best-ever score has been. They're less likely to be interested in your biggest-ever match play victory as it's immeasurable and irrelevant.

MATCH PLAY

We all spend too many tiring hours at work every week trying to make figures look good to want to put ourselves through the same thing every weekend on the golf course. Golf shouldn't be a stress-compounding hobby, but rather a stress-relieving one – a chance to forget life's drudgery and spend a few hours doing what we enjoy doing with our golfing chums.

Yes, we may need to play the odd stroke play round to maintain our handicaps or occasionally test our games under the insidious pressure of the uncompromising scorecard. But who really wants to do that week in, week out? There can be few sadder sights than the golfer who insists on 'keeping a score' while chopping his way in and out of the undergrowth. 'Was that a nine I had there?' he'll say. 'No, I think you three-putted for a ten,' you reply, looking over your shoulder to see the entire course backing up behind you.

Thankfully golf has a perfect antidote in match play, where each hole is its own mini-competition and the total score becomes irrelevant. All you're trying to do is beat your opponent's nett score on every hole. It's golf at its most forgiving and fun, even more so in its popular four-ball better-ball format, which pits two against two with only each pair's better score counting. Here you can throw in the odd big number, and if your partner happens to play the same hole well – dovetailing or 'ham-and-egging it' as it's commonly known – you might still emerge victorious.

Individual stroke play affords you no such luxuries. Does this sound familiar? After a tough week at work you're really looking forward to your weekend round. Your partners suggest stroke play for a couple of quid, and you agree. You start brightly and are still a couple under handicap with four to play. Then disaster strikes. Out of bounds twice, a couple of duffs, a poor chip and of course the obligatory three-putt to round things off. Suddenly you're marking an 11 down on your card. You drop a few more as you limp home and your mood is decidedly black as you sit in the bar staring vacantly into space, wondering just why you put yourself through it. Come Monday morning, you're back in the office with only the ignominy of another round that slipped away to remember your precious weekend by.

But what if you'd played exactly the same golf in a friendly four-ball better-ball? Chances are you'd have been a few up by the 15th thanks to your solid early play, and your partner may well have saved you on that hole. Still up with three to play and at one with the world, you wouldn't have let one bad hole darken your mood. Better still, you'd probably have picked up midway through your nightmare 15th anyway so wouldn't actually have an ugly, stark 11 playing games with your mind. You'd go on to close out the match, then sit down afterwards, taking the mickey out of each other and putting the world to rights over a beer or two.

Sure, let stroke play have its occasional moment, but otherwise stick to match play. Life is just too short and it will help keep the game in perspective, prove a lot more fun and make you better company for your golfing chums. A win, win, win scenario!

16

DRIVING vs
PUTTING

When it comes to the skills required in golf, driving and putting are at opposite ends of the spectrum. Unfortunately most amateurs tend to be proficient at either one or the other, not both. If it came to a straight choice, would you rather be long and straight off the tee or deadly with the flat-stick?

DRIVING

Two shots at the culmination of the 1970 Open Championship at St Andrews demonstrated golf's split personality. Playing in the last group Doug Sanders had a 2-foot putt on the 18th green to claim a deserved victory over Jack Nicklaus. He settled over it and froze. Nerves had taken hold. He delayed for what seemed an eternity before yipping it past the edge. The miss meant a tie with the Golden Bear. This was golf at its worst, its most unfair and frustrating. After four days of intense concentration and superb gritty competitiveness it all came down to a silly little tap that narrowly missed.

The following 18-hole play-off was a close affair and came down to the final hole. One ahead, Nicklaus famously peeled off his sweater, stepped up to the ball and hit one of golf's most audacious shots. A huge drive that ran right on to, and through, the green. The ensuing birdie won him the title. This cavalier shot epitomised everything great about golf, a glorious and brave strike that received the result it deserved. In an ironic twist Sanders then holed an irrelevant birdie putt of roughly the same length as the one he'd missed the previous day.

Golf is about hitting a ball to a target – a putting green. Upon reaching that slick surface the sport of golf finishes and the sport of putting begins. Tapping it about a green isn't golf, it's more like modified croquet. You'll often hear someone described thus: 'He's a great golfer, he just can't putt.' When have you ever heard someone say, 'Oh, he's a great putter, he just can't play golf'? Never. This is because putting is not such an admired or difficult skill as driving. In order to be a great driver, the player must practise hard and have a solid, powerful and rhythmic swing that repeats effectively. When putting, people use all manner of crazy means to get the ball in the hole – stabbing, crouching, using a long wand or a sawn-off blade. There's no rhyme or reason to it, any old hacker can hole a lucky putt.

Here's another reason why putting is ludicrous – a booming 300-yard drive struck sweetly with a perfect touch of draw ending in the centre of the fairway is one single magnificent stroke of golf. Compare it to this – a 3-foot par putt hits an unexpected spike mark and deviates slightly left; the ball hits the edge of the cup, dips into the hole but grabs the lip like a stunt motorbike rider on a wall of death; it accelerates around the back of the cup and ends its journey still above ground. The forced tap-in from half an inch is also one single stroke, albeit 299.99 yards shorter. Far from being magnificent, it's about as irritating as golf gets – unjust and ridiculous.

With your ball on the tee and the fairway stretching in front, you are in control of your destiny. If you make a solid swing with good aim, the ball will travel to the desired spot – enjoyable and fair. With your ball 3 feet above the cup on a spike-marked green, you're not in complete control. When you start it rolling there's a large element of chance as to whether it goes in – not fun and not fair.

PUTTING

You may have heard putting referred to as the 'game within a game'. Well, it's highly likely this phrase first passed the lips of a golfer singularly inadequate in this skilled art form and simply unable to accept that every shot counts the same whether the ball travels an inch or 350 yards. Better, he must have thought, to dismiss putting as a separate entity rather than accept it as the integral part of golf it actually is.

A stranger to the practice green, you would most likely have found him pounding ball after ball away on the range to the admiring gasps of other golfers mistakenly equating ball-crunching distance with golfing proficiency. They would all no doubt be arguing that the exquisite timing and skill required to propel the ball huge distances in a straight line somehow make a good driver of the ball more of a golfer than one highly adept at getting it underground quickly at the far end of the hole.

But ponder this – how often do you see professional golfers fist-pumping or jumping around excitedly after splitting the fairway with a long, arrow-straight drive? Then fast-forward to the putting green. It's a different story there. We all have our own favourite memories – perhaps Sam Torrance holding his arms aloft as his putt dropped to bring the Ryder Cup home to Europe for the first time in 28 years, or Jack Nicklaus chasing down putt after putt on the back nine at Augusta in 1986.

If you're still not convinced of the relative merits of putting and driving, imagine the following scenario. You strike a majestic boomer down the centre. Your opponent sends one clattering into the trees. He chips out still short of you and, unable to reach, lays up to pitching distance. You strike a towering 5-iron to 15 feet. He chips weakly to about 30 feet and the hole is yours . . . or is it? With a beautiful roll he strokes his ball firmly into the centre of the cup. Slightly flustered at no longer having three for it you leave your first putt 3 feet short. You look across. No concession! Suddenly it looks more like 6 feet . . . and is that a spike mark there on your line? One tentative prod later, the ball remains above ground and you both walk off with the same score. To compound your misery, as you walk to the next tee he turns and says, 'That was stroke index 5 so I had a shot there. My hole, I believe.'

Which shot proved more telling – your 300-yarder into position 'A' or his 30-footer? No need to answer. But how many golfers fail to see, or refuse to acknowledge, just how important putting is? Perhaps they're in denial. It's all so unfair, they say. I'm the one playing proper golf. Really? So just what constitutes 'proper golf'?

Let's answer that with a quick look inside any clubhouse in Britain. At the bar are a couple of big-hitting youngsters bragging about just how phenomenally long they are. Over in the corner, quietly supping his pint, sits an old boy whose name can be found on every honours board because he learned from an early age that a good putter is a match for anyone. Now who would you rather draw in the club knockout?

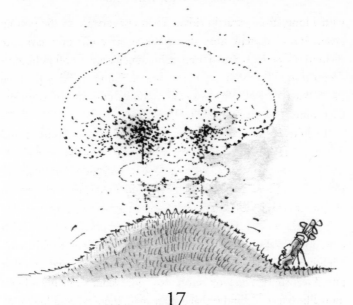

17

50-YARD BUNKER SHOT vs FLOP SHOT OFF A BARE LIE

Sometimes a round of golf can feel like you're tackling the 12 labours of Hercules as you find yourself in one seemingly impossible position after another. But when it comes down to it, which is the toughest shot in golf? Two of the top contenders must be the 50-yard bunker shot and the flop shot off a bare lie.

50-YARD BUNKER SHOT

If it's scary enough to strike the fear of God into even the most seasoned tour pro, the 50-yard bunker shot is comfortably good enough for top honours (with distinction) in any 'toughest shot in golf' debate.

Put the average tour pro in any normal greenside bunker or fairway trap in a half-decent lie and you'll barely discern a flicker in heart rate or perspiration level as they step nonchalantly down into the sand before despatching the ball with contemptuous ease. Modern equipment and techniques mean these shots are bread and butter to them, with those bunkers now hazards in name rather than nature.

But plonk them in a fairway bunker 50 yards out and it's a different story. Whereas from a similar distance on the fairway they'd be expecting a high up-and-down success rate, from the sand they're usually happy to take three and move on.

If the shot is that hard for them, imagine how taxing it is for us, who find the 50-yard pitch tough enough from a perfect lie, let alone a bed of unpredictable sand. It demands the precision and control of a neurosurgeon if you're to avoid the disastrous consequences of the duff or the rapier-like thin that threatens to prematurely end the playing career of anyone foolish enough to venture on ahead to the rashly perceived sanctuary of the green. Little wonder we approach it with pounding heart, sweaty palms and that sense of foreboding you get when setting sail into choppy waters and gathering gloom.

Even from a good lie, it demands everything we typically lack in abundance – first and foremost, more precise contact than any other shot. You simply must get ball, not sand, first and simply must strike it right at the bottom. To compound the complexity, you'll also be employing the kind of half-to-three-quarter-swing many of us find so bewilderingly perplexing. Precision and control of the very highest order are essential for perfect execution.

But it's not over yet. Supposing, just supposing, the planets align for a moment, and everything comes together perfectly in terms of both strike and control. Even then there's another problem. Execute this shot well and your ball will at best stop on a sixpence, and at worst jump back like Dracula recoiling from a boldly held crucifix. You will almost certainly have failed to factor this in and will have played for the front of the green, assuming it will release like all your other shots. So you watch in frustration as your ball either pulls up abruptly in three-putt country or fizzes back, forcing you to get up and down to avoid the dreaded double.

For these reasons, and the fact that most tour pros cite this as golf's toughest test, when you do play one of these exquisitely well, you're quite within your rights to raise your club or doff your cap to the imaginary crowd and bask in the satisfying glow of an almost impossible job well done. Tiger himself would struggle to play this shot any better, and for just one fleeting moment you will have achieved godlike golfing status.

FLOP SHOT OFF A BARE LIE

There are a few things in life that should, and do, scare the pants off the majority of the population – swimming in the sea after watching the film *Jaws*, taking off or landing in high winds and Gillian McKeith, for example. But golfers will agree these things pale into insignificance compared to the sheer terror you'll experience when confronted with a delicate pitch shot over a pot bunker from a tight lie.

As you wander to where your slightly misjudged approach shot has finished, a feeling of panic suddenly grips you. You look at your ball and analyse the lie – it's sitting on a piece of ground that could only be described as mud. *Oh no*, you think. *It's going to be bloody difficult to catch it cleanly from there.* The situation looks bleak, but things take a turn for the even worse when you look at what's between you and the hole. Five yards ahead is a gaping bunker with the pin sitting just over the top of it. There's no question about it: you're about to face the toughest shot in golf. The margins for error are absolutely minute, with all manner of potentially disastrous outcomes.

Make contact a little too high up and you'll skull it; the ball will either fire into the bunker face, or just clear it and career through the green, inevitably into a devilish bunker or some other frightful hazard. You can quickly find yourself racking up a pretty impressive number. Well, impressive if you were opening at the Oval.

If the smallest grain of doubt creeps into your mind about a flop shot over sand, you've had it. You'll decelerate harder than Lewis Hamilton entering the pit lane. The leading edge of your wedge will catch the ground and the ball will travel exactly five yards straight into the trap. Unfortunately it will have gained a little altitude so it'll probably plug, making the next shot extremely difficult as well.

In a worst-case scenario, you'll realise at the last moment you're going to duff the shot and race your hands through impact to try and force the ball over the sand. The club head will catch up with the ball and make contact with it again. Not only will you now be plugged in a bunker but you'll also have incurred a penalty shot for the double hit. If you don't have sweat pouring down your back as you're reading this, you're a better man than most.

The 50-yard bunker shot is a tough one, no question about it. But in comparison to the flop shot over sand from a tight lie it's a picnic. Simply catch the ball clean with a half-swing and watch it check up by the pin. It's a shot you have to commit to with an aggressive swing; it doesn't require the deftness of touch a flop shot demands and the potential repercussions of failure aren't nearly so great.

18
WIND vs
CALM ON A LINKS

The majority of golfers relish the opportunity to play on one of Britain's superb links courses. But invariably a round at the seaside means tackling a howling gale. The question is, do we embrace the breeze or yearn for one of those rare days when there's not a breath of wind?

WIND

Playing links golf on a becalmed day is a little like eating a plain bacon sandwich, watching Christopher Dean skate solo, or settling down alone, Pinot Grigio and chocolates in hand, to watch a weepy movie – all perfectly pleasant in their own way, but without the vital ingredients of HP Sauce, Jayne Torvill or a gorgeous blonde that turn them into something really special.

Yes, your scoring on a calm day may – or may not – be better. But robbed of the full seaside experience, even if it is, you will merely be deluding yourself as to your true capability on the links.

We're not talking about a full-blown gale here either (where the scorecard becomes an irrelevance and the last man standing wins). We're talking about anything from a stiff breeze to a three-to-four-club wind in which waterproofs and trousers flap wildly, the ocean roars loudly and your ball barely stops still on firm, close-cropped greens.

Links golf on these days is what the game is all about. It asks fresh questions of you at every turn, and you get to discover how many of the answers you really have up your sleeve. Can you take full advantage of those 350-yard downwind drives, or do you merely leave yourself impossible downwind pitches over fearsome bunkers to rock-hard greens? Are you man enough to sometimes pull a 4-iron from 120 yards or the big stick on 180-yard par 3s? Can you find the low punch in a rarely accessed corner of your locker as you seek to control ball flight into the wind? Do you have the guts to occasionally start a left-to-right putt right of the hole because you know the wind could make it move the wrong way? Can you execute crisply struck shots and chips from tight turf when the wind is strong enough to throw you off balance?

If links golf in the calm were to be likened to a game of draughts, in the wind it would be more like chess. The playing board remains the same, but the latter game requires a more refined strategy. Seasoned, embattled links campaigners will always take parkland softies to checkmate in next to no time on blowy days because they know all the right moves. And that goes for the mental side too, especially on an out-and-back layout where they'll know not to get too complacent as they turn into the teeth of the wind for the gruelling homeward nine, healthy scorecard in hand.

Enjoy the luxury of wind-free days on the links by all means, but don't allow them to flatter you unduly. They're about as rare as hen's teeth, and by the seaside your game will invariably require considerably more than their gentle test demands. It is only when the wind is really blowing that you will learn whether you're a golfing man up to the rigours of the challenge, or a golfing mouse barely able to squeak by.

CALM

Any connoisseur of Britain's famed links courses will tell you the best time to play one of our great seaside layouts is either dawn or dusk. It's not that they're antisocial people trying to avoid other golfers. It's just that as the sun is rising or in the crepuscular twilight the wind is at its least intense and, as a result, the links at its most enjoyable.

There's no finer place to play golf anywhere in the world than on a British links layout in benign conditions. Imagine – it's warm enough for shirtsleeves as the sun shines across the rolling fairways, defining the humps and swales; a skylark calls out and a lolloping hare makes a break from his hiding place and bounds across in front of you; the gorse is in bloom and the rough is filled with an abundance of wildflowers. You're able to take a moment to appreciate this wonderful scene as you're not being battered by an incessant gale, trudging along with your head down just trying to make it round.

Aficionados of course design will enjoy a calm day on the links so much more as they'll experience the layout in an unadulterated state. They'll see how the holes play without the effect of a tiresome head or tailwind. A 445-yard par 4 will play its length rather than being either unreachable in two or being reduced to a drive and a flick. Cross-bunkers at 270 yards will definitely be in play and a 200-yard par 3 will be testing but fair.

A strong wind can totally ruin your enjoyment of a great links course. Imagine securing your dream game on the Old Course at St Andrews only to find Hurricane Hildebrandt rolling in from the North Sea. After six holes your swing has been beaten within an inch of its life, and the scorecard that was ripped from your hand on the 3rd tee was still climbing as it passed over Cupar. As you watch another drive travel about 105 yards you wonder if this was £130 wisely spent.

You just can't play sensible links golf when the wind is really gusting. Into the wind you try to manufacture any sort of knock-down shot, but every club you use balloons and spends the second half of its flight travelling back towards you. It's exhausting. When the wind is behind and the ground is firm the ball will travel inordinate distances and the greens become virtually impossible to hold.

Then there's the dreaded crosswind. You stand on a tee with a gale blowing off the left. You always hit a bit of a cut anyway so calculate you have to aim the shot 30 yards left over a sea of gorse to have any chance of the ball holding the fairway. You hit it exactly where you intended, but at that very moment the wind dies and your ball soars dead straight into the bushes – infuriating.

Benign and playable conditions that afford you the chance to experience all that is great about the links, or a tiring and frustrating struggle through an unremitting wind that totally changes the character of the course? There's simply no debate.

19
CRAZY GOLF vs
PITCH AND PUTT

Given the choice, most golfers would spend every moment of their spare time out on the links. But family commitments mean it's not always possible. Don't worry, though, there are other options for getting your golfing fix – crazy golf and pitch and putt for example. Which of these best scratches the itch?

CRAZY GOLF

Amble along the prom at any popular British seaside resort and among the amusement arcades, bandstands and fish and chip shops you'll invariably stumble across an 'Arnold Palmer Crazy Golf

Course' or some such establishment. Arnie, of course, will never have set foot on it to painstakingly work out where the windmill might have maximum strategic impact, but even so, it's a far wiser choice for a spot of holiday fun than the adjacent pitch and putt.

The problem with pitch and putt is that it's just too damn close to the real thing for comfort. Playing surfaces will be poor and patchy, hole lengths will typically be the ones over which you're least proficient, and yet non-golfing friends will still expect you to perform. 'You play a bit, don't you?' they say. 'Show us the way.'

'OK,' you say, at first bullishly. But your confidence drains away as you take hold of a 30-year-old pitching wedge with perished grip, a putter best described as a lump of battered metal on the end of a stick, and a rubber ball with several chunks missing. On your first shot the wedge slips from your grasp, your ball shoots off at right angles, and your friend shoots you an amazed 'I thought you played this game' look.

Things go from bad to worse. Dodgy surfaces and an unwieldy weapon nullify your usually strong putting, and to rub salt into the wound, your friend – who knows no different – turns out to be a natural with both wonky wedge and pitted putter. Your humiliation is complete when he tots up the final scores and declares, 'I don't believe it. My first ever game and I've beaten you.'

To avert such embarrassing scenarios, bypass the pitch and putt booth and walk straight up to the crazy golf counter. Putter and ball will be equally dire, but it doesn't matter here because everything is so obviously meant to be just a bit of harmless holiday fun. It's far enough removed from real golf for complete dissociation, leaving you free to focus on judging the pace up the helter-skelter, running it cleverly under the watermill or extricating yourself from those painted 'lakes' and 'bunkers'. The only thing to potentially curb your enjoyment is getting stuck behind a giggling, stiletto-heeled six-ball – and even that is not without its merits.

Crazy golf needs to be taken at face value. And at face value all you're trying to do is negotiate windmills, humps, hollows and unfeasible dog-legs that are nothing to do with golf as we know it. Pitch and putt, though, is disconcertingly close to a key element of the real game, instantly putting you under greater pressure to perform. Who needs that on holiday? So when you head off for Torquay or Skegness this summer, opt for half an hour of crazy golf fun and the chance to win another game by ringing the bell on the 19th. You never know, if you have a good old rummage at home you may even unearth a free game ticket from a successful venture in the dim and distant past, thus saving you a few bob to boot.

PITCH AND PUTT

For a true golf lover there can be no contest when it comes to this argument – the pitch and putt wins hands down. It's golf in microcosm and delivers a concentrated test of golf's most difficult element – the short game. Crazy golf is something completely different to our great sport and, even when viewed independently, it's still a lame activity.

Few of us can honestly say our short game is as sharp as we'd like it to be. The majority of amateurs don't practise pitching and chipping as much as they should. In fact, many people reading this probably don't practise at all. But it's here, at the business end of each hole, that scores can be dramatically improved. If you can increase the percentage of times you get up and down from just off the green your scores will tumble.

The pitch and putt is the perfect place to develop these crucial short-game skills. The holes are short (most won't stretch further than 100 yards) so you'll only need to take a selection of wedges and a putter. The greens are small, so you'll look to be far more accurate with your full-wedge shots. When you miss the greens, and you will tend to, you'll face a variety of challenging chips back to the small targets. If you can master getting up and down at your local pitch and putt it will seem a breeze next time you're out on a full course. Regular visits to the pitch and putt will lower your handicap.

For golfers who live in city centres a trip out to the suburbs or countryside for 18 holes will often mean giving up a full day. In many cases this simply isn't practical – work prevents it during the week and other social commitments can make it difficult at the weekend. But in most cities you'll find pitch and putt layouts so you can still get your golfing fix. You can turn up of an evening, scoot round in less than an hour then head home, or to the pub perhaps.

One great thing about the pitch and putt is that you can enjoy a round there with non-golfing pals. You can treat it as a way to improve your short game while they'll enjoy it as an introduction to golf. It'll be a relaxed and informal knockabout with no stuffy secretary or overzealous member to make you feel you're committing some heinous crime.

Crazy golf is depressing. It conjures images of decaying seaside resorts, flaking paintwork, drizzly weather and soggy fish and chips. An overweight, unshaven man wearing a string vest and smoking a Lambert & Butler will hand you a pink rubber ball and something vaguely resembling a putter through the window of his caravan. He'll grunt something at you that means join the back of the queue behind that four-ball of octogenarians and that family of six. You'll waste a valuable hour of your life tapping the ball under windmills and through clowns' mouths – ridiculous.

If you play a round at the pitch and putt you'll enjoy a fun hour of golf condensed; opt for a round of crazy golf and you're just . . . well . . . crazy.

20

CARRYING vs TROLLEYING

What's the best way to transport your clubs and all your assorted golfing paraphernalia around the course – on your back, which allows you to take the shortest route from A to B as you make your way round, or with wheeled assistance that may require the odd detour, but places less strain on back and shoulders?

CARRYING

The debate between carrying your bag and using a trolley really comes down to a question of your age and physical condition. If you're young, fit and able there's absolutely no reason why you shouldn't carry your clubs.

If you use a trolley then either you're not strong enough to carry or you have an injury preventing you from doing so. Given either circumstance it's obviously completely acceptable to use a trolley. Golf is one of the few sports people can continue to enjoy right into their twilight years and trolleys are one of the many innovations that facilitate this.

With this in mind, carrying your clubs shows you are still a physically fit and determined golfer. It gives you a psychological boost and possibly the edge in matches: 'I carry my clubs. That means I can also carry the water at the 16th and will still be going strong as we head up the 18th fairway.'

There are other, more practical, reasons why carrying is better: It speeds up play, as you can take your bag right up to the edge of the green. When you have a trolley you generally have to leave your clubs some distance from the putting surface. This often means people put their caddy carts in completely the wrong place and then take an extra minute or two to fetch them and move on to the next tee.

When there's an elevated tee you don't have to stand at the bottom of the steps debating what clubs you're going to take with you. Simply take the whole bag and decide when you have a proper view of what you have to tackle.

If you and three pals are going away on a day trip, trolleys can make the logistics complicated. If all four are using carry bags you'll probably be able to fit all the kit in one decent-sized boot so you'll only need to take one car. As soon as you add trolleys and trolley bags to the equation boot space is taken up all too quickly. You'll probably require two motors – petrol money doubled.

Trolley bags are very inflexible. If you use one you simply have to get a trolley as the bag is far too cumbersome and heavy to carry. They're also awkward to get in and out of the car and they're too big to fit in most club lockers. If you've picked up an injury or you've decided to go out for a second 18 then it's easy to sling your carry bag on to a hire trolley.

What about going abroad? The carry bag fits easily into a flight bag so it's relatively little trouble to travel with it. It is feasible to take a trolley bag on a golfing holiday but you'll have no extra room in your flight cover, and it'll weigh a metric tonne.

So the choice is either carry your clubs, make life easy for yourself and appear robust, or take a trolley, inconvenience your playing partners and lose the psychological edge. If you've got the physical ability, carry.

TROLLEYING

To clearly illustrate why trolleying is the wiser option, let's head down to the supermarket for the weekly shop. You know it's going to be a pretty big one and you're likely to be in among the Weety Flakes and taramasalata for quite some time, so what do you do? Take a couple of baskets then end up flagging down the frozen food aisle and struggling to even make it to the spotty, monosyllabic teenager at the checkout, or simply load it all into a large trolley that even your five-year-old can push?

Simple, isn't it? And so it should be with your golf if you want to make it safely down the stretch – golf's equivalent of the frozen food aisle – before checking out with the score you deserve, rather than the one you did deserve until you got too weary to be able to properly execute the shots needed to achieve it.

How can it ever make sense to lug around a heavy bag of clubs plus all your associated bits and pieces when the rules allow you to transport that burden around on a set of wheels designed specifically to take the weight off your back? Which other perfectly legal opportunity to optimise their scoring potential do so many golfers spurn quite so glibly?

Perhaps it hails from misplaced machismo and an outdated notion that serious golfers only ever carry. 'None of the low handicap boys at my club would be seen dead using a trolley,' you say. Wouldn't they? Look again – times have changed. Not only will many of them now be on wheels, but also many of their charges will even be of the motorised variety.

If you were on a Himalayan expedition, would you try and go it alone or make the most of the Sherpa help available? Without Tenzing, Hillary may never have hit the headlines quite so dramatically in 1953 and he certainly didn't say to his loyal Sherpa, 'OK, I might get a bit tired nearer the top, but I'm a serious mountaineer so I'll carry everything myself on the final ascent while you take a bit of a breather, Norgay, old boy.'

Plenty of scientific research has probably been carried out to highlight just how many more calories you burn off carrying than trolleying. However, regardless of the exact figures you don't need a boffin to tell you that you'll use up far more energy walking 4 miles with 20-odd kilos on your back than without. But then, what are you playing golf for – to burn off the flab or make the best possible score?

Assuming it is the latter, let's finish off with something vaguely approaching humour. The golfer who insists on rejecting wheeled assistance must surely be off his 'trolley' and should indeed be 'carried' off by the men in white coats to the nearest sanatorium. OK, the humour may be debatable, but the sentiment most definitely is not.

It's my lucky glove -

21

LEATHER vs ALL-WEATHER GLOVES

There are a bamboozling number of choices when selecting golf equipment but, when it comes to the glove, there's just one principal decision to be made – leather or all-weather. The leather glove delivers comfort and style while the all-weather option provides durability and versatility. Which virtues are more important?

LEATHER

Like a vintage Margaux, a Cuban cigar or a weekend in St Tropez, the leather golf glove is one of the finer things in life. It oozes class and golfing style. It's the choice of all top quality golfers and a clear sign that you know what you're doing on the links.

The all-weather glove is not one of the finer things in life. Using the same analogy, it's a bottle of house red, a *Café Crème* or a weekend in Benidorm. It may well do the job but it'll get there without even a modicum of elegance.

Watching golf on the television, how many top players do you see using synthetic gloves? Not many. The pros have their pick of golf equipment and when it comes to hand-wear they choose leather. This is because the leather glove is like a second skin, offering maximum comfort and feel as well as excellent grip.

The all-weather mitt does provide grip and it is more durable than leather, but this durability comes at a price. With all-weather you get about as much feel as if you were wearing a pair of gardening gloves. In fact, their similarity to gardening gloves might be quite useful, as you'll probably find yourself in the shrubbery quite often because you'll be gaining absolutely no feedback on the quality or direction of your strikes through the super-thick synthetic fabric.

Consider this, would you use a sub-standard ball? Would you be prepared to tee up a *DDH 500* in the Saturday Medal? No. So why would you be happy to don a sub-standard glove? A silky smooth, ice-white, clean leather glove inspires confidence. It gives you the sensation that, 'Yes, I am a golfer and I can go out and shoot a low score.' The all-weather glove is a sign that you're not confident with your game, 'No I probably won't play well today but at least my glove should come out of it unscathed.'

OK, so the leather glove may be a couple of quid more expensive than an all-weather one, but how much are you prepared to pay to get the most out of your game? Most of us won't balk at paying hundreds for clubs, bags and shoes. In the grand scheme of golfing expenditure, the difference between a £9.99 all-weather glove and a £13, superbly fitting, soft leather beauty is pretty inconsequential.

The all-weather glove has its place – in the bag in case of a torrential downpour. But that's the extent of its usefulness. Leather is the choice of the professionals and will inspire you to play more confident and better golf; in addition, you'll gain extra feel and a clearer idea of how you're striking the ball. On top of all these practical benefits, you'll also look a good deal more stylish than those all-weather wearing amateurs.

ALL-WEATHER

You know the scenario. You get to the course only to find you've either forgotten your glove or your dog-eared one has finally, and irretrievably, given up the ghost. There's no two ways about it – you're going to have to invest in a new one. You pop into the shop, where the pro rubs his hands in glee and points you towards a rack of gleaming white soft cabretta leather gloves. But there's a problem – the prices are making your eyes hurt, and you just know that the way you get through them you're going to be back here in a month going through the same process. Good news for the pro; bad news for your bank balance.

So should you feel in any way stigmatised or less of a golfer if you opt for one of the more appealingly-priced all-weather options the pro will reluctantly eventually show you? Absolutely not, for several reasons.

First, what are you really sacrificing? Admittedly, a little feel and that disturbingly sensuous experience of leather on palm. But beyond that, you're also kissing goodbye to: glass-like durability, with any minor flaws or movement in your grip rapidly wearing through the wafer-thin leather; a fit that starts off snug but quickly goes all baggy on you; and a vulnerability to water that can render the glove useless after just one little shower – unless you're among that rare breed who meticulously dry it out away from a direct source of heat as soon as you get home. Even then, it's never quite the same, and more likely you'll stuff it in your bag, then rediscover it covered in a strange green mould on your next outing two weeks later. Or your wife will find it and 'helpfully' pop it on a radiator leaving you trying to force on something with a Picasso-esque hand shape and the textural properties of balsa wood next time you play.

No such problems with durable all-weather gloves, which can pretty much take care of themselves. For a start, you'll be quids in at the till, where you can get two, even three for the price of just one leather one. Then, you quite possibly won't need to revisit the pro shop for another year, such are their hard-wearing qualities. That's why pros and manufacturers don't really want to sell them to you – they know they won't be seeing you for a while with all the scope for knock-on sales and chance purchases each visit brings. Some all-weather gloves have vastly improved feel these days too, so you won't be trying to caress delicate shots over bunkers wearing something that feels like a thick woolly mitt. They'll also keep their shape whatever the weather throws at them, and many can even be popped in the washing machine so they'll look pristine again for your next round.

So don't feel any less of a golfer for not succumbing to golf's great cabretta scam. You're giving up very little, and gaining the where-withal to keep yourself stocked up with Pro V1s, or perhaps, over the course of a season, a decent sum towards that new driver you just know is going to transform your game. So forget leather; go all-weather.

22
ACCURACY vs
DISTANCE

Technological advances have enabled the average amateur to hit the ball far greater distances. Many more players can now reach par 5s in two and reduce par 4s to a drive and a pitch. But would you prefer to be firing in a 6-iron from the short grass or a pitching wedge from the thick rough?

ACCURACY

Unerring accuracy has so much more to commend it than mere blast-away distance that it's one of the biggest shames – and indeed myths – of modern golf that distance is all that matters. Monster hitters certainly draw the biggest crowds and attract the most hero worship even though they often don't have a clue how to actually put a score together – another sad sign of our shallow, sensationalist times.

Accuracy is the real name of the game, as golf is ultimately about getting a small ball into a marginally bigger hole anything up to 600 yards away in as few strokes as possible. This is patently not that easy if you're 300-plus yards off the tee, but 100 yards wide in the kind of dense forest from which Japanese Second World War soldiers still occasionally emerge wondering why it's all gone quiet.

Of course, the ultimate golfing combination is both distance and accuracy – then you've got an unbeatable package. But relatively few of the tour's big boomers are also straight enough to take full advantage of their prodigious hitting. There'll be similar types at your club too, usually talking very loudly about exactly how far they hit it or how little club they hit into certain holes. Ask them what they actually scored though and their reply is likely to drop several decibels to an indiscernible mumble, because somehow they've deluded themselves that distance is of all-pervading importance. All brawn and no brain – never has 'brute force and ignorance' been a more descriptively accurate analysis.

It's a similar story on tour too. A snapshot of European Tour stats from 2008 showed that of the top 10 for distance, only one finished in the top 100 on the money list while just three retained their cards. That figure goes up by just one for the driving accuracy statistics. But it's when you get to the putting green that things really begin to count. Here, distance counts for nothing and accuracy everything. Eight of the top 10 putters made the top 100 on the money list and among them was double major winner Padraig Harrington.

Accuracy has such an important knock-on benefit on every golf hole that it's hard to understand just how it's become such an underestimated skill. If you're on the fairway, you'll have a better chance of finding the green and exercising some control over your ball on landing. If you do that, you're then putting, which makes par much easier to achieve than if you're forever having to conjure up some greenside magic to get up and down. And if you do the 'fairways and greens' thing often enough, it's inevitable that sometimes you'll convert the birdie chances you generate.

The golfer who regularly finds the short, and then even shorter, grass will virtually always prevail over the erratic bomber, especially at club level where powers of recovery are less advanced than on tour. Consistency, ironically, overpowers power.

So leave the mistakenly lauded machismo to the big-hitting glory boys and concentrate on what really makes you a better golfer – hitting fairways and greens rather than bunkers, trees and occasionally even adjacent properties.

DISTANCE

If you can generate good distance then your timing and the basic mechanics of your swing must be efficient. If you can shift the ball 250 yards off the tee, even if you don't find the fairway too often, you have the potential to be a good golfer. If you hit the ball consistently straight but have never been able to get it to fly more than 120 yards then you're never going to be a single-figure handicapper. Accuracy can be developed but distance is something fundamental to the game of golf. For that reason, if you were forced to make a choice between distance and accuracy then distance would have to get the nod.

The key to the long ball lies in knowing when to use it. Having the monster drive up your sleeve for the wide-open par 5 is a huge boon. What a bonus it is for those who have the length to reach the average par 5 in two or maybe even drive the short par 4. But being able to drop down to a fairway wood or long iron on the tighter holes is equally advantageous. Where the shorter man is forced to hit driver to bring the green in range for his approach, the distance merchant can afford to play more cautiously from the tee. If he does decide to let one rip he can shift it much closer to the putting surface. It's far easier to approach a green with a pitching wedge than a 4-iron.

It may seem superficial but there's no denying that hitting a huge drive feels great. The massive adrenalin rush as you spank the ball away is hard to beat. The good feeling is sustained as you walk an extra 30 yards past your playing partners' efforts before reaching your drive. It's a good way to demoralise your opponent in match play. Make a point of saying 'good drive' as they bunt one down the middle. They'll feel a warm glow until you skelp one 50 yards further.

You can make a name for yourself with prodigious hitting. People will spot you across the fairway and comment to their playing partner, 'There's the fellow who hits the impressive ball.' It's great for self-confidence on the course. You're less likely to be recognised as 'that chap who hits it rather poorly but manages to keep it on the fairway more often than not'.

What about the professional arena – surely accuracy off the tee is a prerequisite there? In fact, it isn't. Vijay Singh, Tiger Woods and Phil Mickelson have been three of the world's best players over the last decade. They finished the 2008 season 1st, 2nd and 3rd respectively on the PGA Tour money list. But they ended the year 150th, 169th and 181st in the driving accuracy stats. Not very easy to draw a direct correlation, is it? So what do they have in common? Well, they've all featured in the upper reaches of the driving distance statistics throughout their careers. It seems distance rather than accuracy spawns success.

23

PUTTERS: BLADE vs MALLET

A classic, sleek-looking blade that demands the user has a deft touch and smooth stroke, or a state-of-the-art mallet designed scientifically to give you every possible assistance on the putting green? One's tricky to master but looks great; the other's easy to use but looks awful. Which is best?

BLADE

On the eve of the 1923 US Open Bobby Jones was putting poorly. A friend suggested he might have the solution – an old putter he turned to in times of need. It was a simple offset blade with a hickory shaft, forged by Condie and sold by William Winton. The putter was almost 20 years old and had the nickname 'Calamity Jane' stamped on the back.

Jones tried Calamity Jane and loved the feel. He used it and won. In fact, he used the original then a replica (Calamity Jane II) to win all 13 of his major titles.

The classic bladed putter has been the weapon of choice for the game's greats for over 100 years. Palmer, Nicklaus and Player all played with a bladed putter.

Think of a couple of the best putters in recent times:

- *Ben Crenshaw.* The Texan's father bought 'Gentle Ben' a Wilson 8802 blade in Harvey Penick's shop when Ben was just a teenager. Crenshaw used that putter, 'Little Ben', to win 17 PGA Tour events and two Masters.
- *Phil Mickelson.* Probably the best feel putter of the last 15 years. His choice of flat-stick? You've got it: the blade. He's had a few models over the years, but whichever manufacturer is providing his kit, he always opts for a bladed putter head.

Putting is all about touch and feel. From 40 feet, across a fast-running and sloping surface you must rely on judgement and good hands to get the ball somewhere near the cup. The blade is by far the best option for doing this. A well-made bladed putter will feel like an extension of your arms and hands. You'll really get that sensation of rolling the ball towards the hole.

How are you supposed to get any sort of feel for the greens when you're wielding something that looks more like a branding iron? The mallet is an ugly and cumbersome excuse for a putter that should be looked down upon rather than revered.

A sleek and stylish blade is the putting equivalent of an Aston Martin DB5 – if you're seen in control of one you look damn cool and people envy you. It's a beautiful and responsive piece of equipment that performs with grace and authority. A clunky and unsightly mallet is the Renault Espace of putters – a clumsy brute that arouses pity rather than envy. Barely responsive at all and lacking in any sort of performance, it may get you from A to B, but it will do it without even a modicum of style or flair.

Ben Sayers once said, 'A good player who is a great putter is a match for anyone.' To be a truly great putter you must groove a perfect stroke and be able to repeat it. The best way to do that is by learning to wield a classic blade putter with skill and finesse. Find the perfect blade and you'll stay with it for life.

MALLET

In principle, this is the blade versus cavity back argument revisited, yet for some strange reason, the mass exodus from blade to mallet putter has been nowhere near as much of a stampede as the one from blade to perimeter-weighted iron.

But if something claimed to help you roll the ball more consistently towards the target – as mallet putters do – just why would you spurn its benefits? It appears there may be a residual stubbornness when it comes to the putting green, and a misguided attitude that says, 'Who really needs help there? All you've got to do is roll the ball along the ground; how can one style of putter be any better or worse than another?'

If this were Stephen Fry's *QI* television programme, this would be the point at which the alarm would sound for an answer everyone assumes to be true, but which is actually a myth. For while you do indeed roll a ball along the ground, that is only half the story – you also have to get it into a hole measuring just $4\frac{1}{4}$ inches across. Think of it like that and the relative margin for error is considerably less than on a shot to a green measuring perhaps 30 yards across, or to a fairway where you can often miss the dead centre by 20 yards either side and still be OK.

The reason the mallet is more fit for purpose than a blade is the greater moment of inertia and stability its head design offers. With extra weight further from the face and often in extreme corner locations, the extent to which the putter will twist on off-centre contact is reduced sufficiently for mishits to maintain more of their intended line, thus either dropping or leaving you a nonchalant tap-in rather than a nervy knee-trembler. So three becomes two more often, two becomes one more often, and your scores start heading in the right direction.

When you add in the built-in targeting aids that many large-headed mallets boast, courtesy of vivid markings and graphics on top, there should be fewer misses on the grounds of misdirection too.

If this all sounds like cheating, in some ways it is – but in a perfectly legitimate way thanks to a legal loophole. For while the rules state that a putter should be 'plain in shape', the strict definition of that is a little vague, with some modern designs prompting the question: 'How on earth could that be construed as plain?' But once the R&A had deemed Odyssey's phenomenally successful 2-Ball OK, it really opened the floodgates, for few putter designs could really be any less plain than that.

So shrewd golfers have latched on to them and started using these modern weapons to launch serious assaults on their putting stats and handicaps at the end of the hole where improvement doesn't necessarily demand radical swing surgery – just the best tool for the job. True, even the most technologically advanced army may not win all the time. But the correlation is too high to take any unnecessary chances. When it comes to the battle for supremacy on the greens, mallets win over blades every time, which is why you should arm yourself with one.

24

WINTER GOLF vs HANGING UP THE CLUBS

When the leaves start to fall and those lazy, hazy, crazy days of summer turn first to autumn, then to winter, do real golfers simply lock their clubs in the shed and take up alternative indoor pursuits for four months, or battle on bravely through freezing, wet, windswept conditions on courses often barely fit for purpose?

WINTER GOLF

Britain's winter golfers are a brave and noble breed. They follow in the tradition of our country's great adventurers – Raleigh, Cook and Shackleton. In clubhouses up and down the UK the midwinter golfer can be heard echoing the words of Captain Lawrence Oates as he prepares to forge out into a sleet-filled gale: 'I'm just going outside and may be some time.' Such men are the heroes of our sport – a dedicated and passionate band of champions with a never-say-die attitude. The fair-weather player who hangs up his clubs for winter is not a true golfer. These scaredy-cats should stick to croquet, cricket or some other summer-only activity, as golf is a year-round sport. Can you imagine Old Tom Morris refusing a game on the links because it looked a bit parky out? Certainly not. If you really love the game, how could you go for months at a time without swinging a club?

Battling through everything the weather can throw at you and still recording a score is one of the most rewarding achievements in golf. It's a true test of your grit and determination and you must learn a multitude of different shots to counter the conditions – the low punch into the January wind or the runner that scampers across a frozen fairway to find an icy winter green. You must learn to pick the ball cleanly off a muddy lie and to stroke the ball across greens more reminiscent of a Conference League penalty area than a putting surface. But all these strange shots will serve you in good stead when the weather turns for the better. Imagine how easy that pitch from a perfect lie will feel or how confident you can be over a 6-footer knowing there are no tussocks or divots on your line.

If you want to improve your golf you simply must play through the winter. Not only because you learn to deal with a plethora of different scenarios but also because a five-month lay-off every year will set you back. How can you expect to return to the game stronger in March when you haven't seen a fairway since October? You often hear people say, 'A break is good, it gives you a chance to forget all the mistakes that have crept in.' Yes, but you've also forgotten how to hit the ball. You don't see Butch Harmon recommending Adam Scott takes six months off because he might just be better when he comes back.

Relatively few people are aware of the joys of winter golf. It's a great secret for those who stick at it. You can walk straight on to the course without even having to book a time and then enjoy a peaceful round that takes less than 3 hours. And on that perfect sunny, crisp day when there's not a breath of wind, you've really hit the jackpot. How good that post-round pint tastes as you smugly consider what the summer-only golfers are missing out on.

HANGING UP CLUBS

Is it better to soldier on bravely through the winter or put the clubs away until warmer times return? Let's take a lead on this from the animal kingdom where those that *can* hibernate *do*, because there's nothing worth staying awake for and they need to recharge their batteries for the following spring. Sound familiar?

Golf is a game best played with the sun on your back, verdant fairways underfoot, herbaceous and arboreal surroundings in full bloom, and on greens that are more akin to luxury carpets than sheets of crumpled paper. Wise golfers know winter is the ideal time to take a break, switch to indoor activities for a while, and spend some time getting their golf gear and club line-up sorted for next season.

Don't be fooled by the tours who simply follow the sun for year-round summer golf. If you're confined to a small corner of our seasonally vulnerable isles it's simply not like that for you – take a look out the window. And if you have been seduced by the pictures beamed into your living room from some warm golfing haven on the other side of the planet, here are a few stark reminders as to why your clubs should be sent into an enforced four-month hibernation every year.

Winter days can be bitingly cold, demoralisingly wet, ferociously windy or even play-stoppingly snowy (or any combination of the four). You'll be wading through mud and casual water for 4 hours, unless the ground is frozen solid, in which case you'll have to suffer the indignity of watching beautifully flighted approaches twang off the greens into Farmer Giles's field like those rubber balls from your youth – that's if the hypersensitive greenkeeper hasn't closed the course.

Your ball will run nowhere on landing, leaving more lengthy approaches than your long game is really up to. If you catch it heavy you'll pebbledash yourself with mud and debris, and if you catch it thin you'll lose all sensation in your fingertips for days to come. You'll have to wear a stupid hat to keep warm, and spend hours cleaning your shoes after every round. And a couple of decent pairs of trousers will eventually bite the dust when even Daz can no longer cope with the ground-in grime.

Tees will be miles forward so you're only playing half a golf course anyway, and greens will either be awful or, worse still, of the temporary variety perched on some unfeasible slope. Perhaps the ultimate winter golf deterrent is the patronising bucket hole. When the committee decides you need holes the size of dustbin lids to have any chance, it's no longer golf as we know it and high time to do something else until normality returns.

If there's anything in this exhaustive list that's got you itching to get the clubs out between November and February then you're beyond help. For most right-thinking golfers it will merely have served to confirm that locking the clubs away in the shed for four months is indeed the only sensible course of action.

25

18-HOLERS vs
9-HOLERS

Many 9-holers harbour ambitions of one day growing to the full 18.
Many have already taken the plunge in a bid to boost their standing in
the game. But with mounting pressures on time and money, could it be
that 9-holers actually hold certain advantages in today's world? This
debate addresses the relative merits of each.

18-HOLERS

The earliest golf courses had varying numbers of holes. Leith and
Bruntsfield Links had 5 and Musselburgh had 7. The Old Course at
St Andrews had 12 holes of which 10 were played twice so there

were, effectively, 22 holes. In 1857 second holes were put into the eight double greens of the Old Course, creating a round of 18 holes. In 1858 the St Andrews Club stipulated a round of 18 holes for matches between its own members.

Today, the vast majority of golf courses across the world are 18 holes including very nearly, if not all, the most famous layouts used for professional and elite amateur tournaments. Golf is now played over 18 holes in the same way tennis is played on a court that's 78 feet long and 27 feet wide or snooker on a table measuring 11 feet 8 inches by 5 feet 10 inches. As golf is inextricably linked to 18 holes in this way, it would be very strange if a course was anything but 18 holes long. Unfortunately there is a stunted and inferior option that sprang up where there was insufficient land for 18 holes or when a club was low on funds – the dreaded 9-holer.

Most golfers unfortunate enough to visit a 9-hole course have every intention of playing round twice – to complete their 18 holes and, thereby, return a meaningful score. But how dull it is to have to play the same holes all over again.

When you visit a proper course for the first time every hole brings a little excitement and expectation. You approach each of the 18 tees feeling anticipation about the next challenge you'll be facing and this is one of the most appealing things about travelling to new courses. If you play a 9-hole layout you're reducing this element of enjoyment by half. Playing the same holes for a second time, there are no surprises as you head into the back nine. You know exactly what's coming and, more often than not, there isn't a great deal to look forward to.

A key problem at a 9-hole course is getting out for your back nine. It's incredibly irritating when you've flown round the first nine without a soul in front of you only to see the last four-ball of a seniors' match teeing off the first as you putt out on the 9th green. You took an hour and 20 minutes to get round the first time but it takes a full hour more for the second loop. Given the back nine is tedious anyway because you've played the holes before, it makes for a rather boring couple of hours.

If you go to the cinema would you prefer to sit down and watch a 2-hour feature or a 1-hour short twice through? If you go for a meal would you prefer a starter and a main course or just to have the same starter twice? If you can honestly say the latter options are more appealing then the 9-hole course would suit you perfectly.

9-HOLERS

If only course developers in the 1980s golf boom had had the foresight to build more 9-holers than prestige golf complexes, the modern breed of time-poor golfer would have been far better served, and the countryside would be less littered with sprawling 18- or 36-hole white elephants, many of which never came close to meeting their original owners' unrealistic aspirations.

Those responsible for these white elephants failed to take into account two key factors – the average golfer's available time and disposable income. The former is under increasing pressure for most, and the latter proved somewhat more fragile than those developers ever envisaged, fluctuating wildly according to the economic climate.

While few really wanted, or could afford, to sign up to those luxury projects, many more latched on to the limited number of 9-holers that sprouted up because they met their time and money needs head on. Not many have unlimited thousands and endless hours to throw at golf; many more have a few hundred pounds and a couple of hours here and there, which is all the average 9-holer requires.

There are a couple of other ways in which the 9-holer scores heavily over the 18-holer, one again to do with time and the other with scoring. The first relates to those occasions when you've only got a couple of hours, but really fancy a knock – perhaps on busy weekends or pleasant summer evenings after work. The 9-holer is perfect then. You can start at the 1st and play round to the 9th in under 2 hours no problem – mission accomplished. On many 18-holers, especially if the 9th lies miles from the clubhouse, you'll face the often fraught task of trying to cut back in on later holes without irritating others. On busy days, this may prove impossible and you'll get to play just four or five holes, before lugging your clubs miles without ever wielding them in anger again as you attempt, un-successfully, to find somewhere to squeeze in a few more en route back to the clubhouse – deeply disheartening and a complete waste of time.

As for the scoring, the 9-holer holds a distinct advantage over the 18-holer when it comes to full-round competitions, as you can use the front nine master-sleuth-style to come up with the ideal strategy for the back nine, where even if the tees aren't quite the same, pin positions will be (other than at the few clubs to adopt the twin-hole system). Any doubts over distances or clubbing will be eliminated as you'll know precisely where the flag is, what club you hit earlier and how well you hit it – all the evidence you need to make a better fist of things second time round. So, your own inconsistency notwith-standing, there really is no excuse for not scoring better on the back nine, giving you greater scope than on an 18-holer to salvage your round, or press on for a really good score. Forewarned is forearmed.

So rather than viewing 9-holers as golf's poor relations, seek out your local one and take full advantage of its time, money and scoring benefits.

26

PLAYING FOR PRIDE vs
PLAYING FOR CASH

For some golfers, the simple delight of playing well is ample reward for their endeavours, whether or not they actually win. For others, such noble ideals are not enough. They only get their golfing kicks when there's money on the line. So should we be playing for pride alone, or the chance to profit at the expense of our rivals?

PLAYING FOR PRIDE

The love of money is the root of all evil, which is why, unless you're a professional, golf should be a game played for pride rather than potential profit. Most of us play with our friends and as soon as you introduce money into the friendship dynamic, you're asking for trouble. With money in the mix, friendships can become strained, especially if one person is regularly profiting at the expense of others, as is often the case in a game of form and confidence.

If your game has gone south, the last thing you need is the certain knowledge that not only are you going to lose, but you're also going to be handing over your hard-earned cash – a double dose of demoralisation that quickly opens the door to resentment. Even worse, there's always someone who's happy to pocket the cash when he's winning, yet all too eager to renege when his touch deserts him. 'Let's just play without anything on the line today; my game's not up to much and if we play for money, I might as well hand it over here and now,' he says, playing with your conscience just as you're thinking, *What about last week when I was chopping it; you were happy to take my money then!*

True, playing for money generates an initial buzz as you con-template just how much you could walk away with. But after a few holes of stunning mediocrity on your part, and a bright start by others, suddenly you're staring down the barrel of a sum that would take some explaining to the other half if she were to get wind of it. *That could have paid for little Quentin's new school shoes*, you can hear her rightfully pained voice shrieking.

So if you want to avoid an awkward silence on the ride home, your best mate's pocket bulging with cash formerly known as yours, stick to playing golf for golf's sake. If you can't take sufficient satisfaction from simply playing well and winning, you're on a slippery slope that threatens to devalue what the game really stands for. Knowing you've done battle with the course, yourself and your fellow competitors and emerged victorious should be more than ample remuneration for your endeavours.

To close, an example to show just why playing for pride should always prevail. Have you ever heard of the innocuous-sounding 'penny a yard' game? The outright winner of any hole pockets a penny for each yard of its length from the other players, with double payouts for winning birdies. Sounds harmless, and normally things even themselves out over 18 holes. But just occasionally someone comes out all guns blazing with an early birdie barrage and suddenly you've done £20 without batting an eyelid. You begin to feel the pressure and further losses inevitably follow as your swing tightens up and your putting stroke deserts you. When it's all over, you've lost too much for a game between friends, creating an awkwardness that ruins the day. And all because the money side has spiralled unexpectedly out of control.

The moral of the tale? If you really value your golfing friendships, play for personal pride alone.

PLAYING FOR CASH

The Rules of Golf contains a 'Policy on Gambling' as an appendix to the section concerning amateur status. This states there is no objection to informal wagering between individuals so long as a number of criteria are met. One of these criteria is that 'the amount of money involved is not generally considered to be excessive'. So for the purposes of this argument 'playing for cash' should be viewed as a game where the bet is significant but not excessive and, more importantly, that those involved in the wager are not set to lose more than they can afford.

OK, that's the formalities out of the way and we can all keep our amateur status. Good.

Seven-time major champion Sam Snead once said, 'If you're not betting while playing golf, you're just walking in a field with another man.' For him, and all those who view golf as a competitive sport, golf and betting go hand in hand. Most of us play golf to try and win and our enjoyment is heightened when we feel a little pressure during a round. In tournaments the pressure of playing to handicap or giving yourself a chance of victory is sufficient to get the competitive juices flowing and the nerve endings tingling. In bounce games, however, you need a little something extra to generate that sensation. A friendly wager will do it nicely. Even if the sum of money is relatively insignificant, the tension you'll feel over that crucial putt for a half is considerably enhanced. It's a great sensation and it makes the feeling of satisfaction/elation when the putt drops so much more intense.

If there's no money on a game you'll just saunter round without a care for your performance. If you lose one out of bounds or leave a putt in the jaws you'll merely shrug your shoulders. It's no way to improve and it's not good preparation for when you have a card in your hand and have to make a score. If you're used to heaping pressure on yourself by betting on bounce games, you'll know how to deal with nerves when it comes to a tough match in the club knockout or when you're sitting on 35 points through 16 holes of the midweek Stableford. Learning to control your nerves is one of the most important skills in golf and placing a little money on bounce games is the perfect training.

One of the great things about betting on a game is that even if you and your opponent are playing dismally, you'll continue to try until the final putt has dropped. There'll be no question of walking off after 12 and you'll be fighting tooth and nail to get ahead or claw back the deficit. You'll continue to compete to the death. Imagine the pleasure when you grind out a win despite playing well below your best. Your golf was poor but you displayed tenacity and determination – important skills for every golfer.

If you're still not convinced and refuse to risk a few quid at next Sunday's roll-up, you should do as Sam Snead advises – put on your hiking sandals, find the nearest field and start rambling.

27
RELAXED vs
STRICT DRESS CODES

Golf is one of the few competitive sports where participants can choose what they wear, but at most clubs this choice is strictly governed by a set of 'dress codes'. Are these guidelines essential to maintain standards and protect the game? Or do they deter youngsters and newcomers, jeopardising the future of our sport?

RELAXED DRESS CODE

Picture this scene: You've just finished a pleasant round and are en route to the bar for post-round refreshment. An old boy dressed in a tatty old pair of grey slacks just short enough to reveal some dirty beige socks approaches you. He's wearing a Pringle jumper, circa 1981, with holes at the elbows, over a rigid-collared, mauve shirt. On his feet are a pair of Velcro loafers you'd normally only see on someone after corrective surgery. He points at your well-fitted and stylish trousers and says, 'No jeans allowed in the clubhouse laddie.'

'Erm. These aren't jeans, they're cotton trousers,' you reply.

'Yes they are jeans – they have a rivet on the pocket. Now go and change them at once,' he snaps. 'And while you're about it, change those trainers.' He waves at your new black leather shoes that have the slightest hint of a sporty design. 'The steward will lend you a pair.'

You amble off with your tail between your legs and return wearing your waterproof trousers and a pair of size-14, tired grey slip-ons that most tramps would be ashamed to be seen in. Yes, you're now adhering to the club's strict dress code, but you look absolutely ridiculous.

Golf clubs that stick resolutely to an old-fashioned dress code are ill-advised and backward-thinking. They must move with the times and accept the days of the Raj are over. Young people no longer wear black tie to dinner. People under the age of 50 have developed a different way of dressing that is no less smart than generations past, just different.

At a time when clubs are looking to attract new young members, telling them they have to dress like their grandpa to go out on the course is not a great marketing ploy.

For those who don't play, golf's image is still one of stuffiness and pretension. Strict dress codes only serve to perpetuate this and it's to the detriment of our great sport.

Shorts throw up a particular problem for the 'stuck in the mud' golf club. At many you'll see the notice: 'Tailored shorts may be worn.' What does this mean? Do you have to go to Savile Row and request that your tailor throw together a pair of half-length chinos? Unless you do that you can generally only buy shorts that are made in factories in the Far East, i.e. not by a tailor.

Then there's the issue of socks. Many clubs insist you accompany shorts with knee-high hosiery, negating any cooling benefits and making you look like an extra from *It Ain't Half Hot Mum*. Others stipulate that short white socks be worn, but how short is a short sock? It's a minefield.

It's still important that some sort of regulations remain. Nobody wants to see people playing golf in swimming trunks or football strips. But the rules should be far more relaxed to allow for changing trends and to attract young people to golf clubs and to the sport in general.

STRICT DRESS CODE

The problem with dress regulations is that if you give the modern breed of 'nobody tells me what to do' golfer an inch he'll take a mile and to hell with everyone else. Maintaining common standards in a largely selfish world is a tough battle, but one well worth fighting for the sake of the qualities our great sport has traditionally fostered, not the least of which is respect.

In a bygone era everyone seemed to dress much more smartly whether at work, at home or out and about, so there's always going to be friction between those used to the standards of yesteryear and those who would take it straight to the unions if their employer asked them to stop dressing in a certain way.

With regard to on-course dress regulations, most golf clubs aren't really too demanding – a collared shirt with a pair of normal trousers. Is that too much to ask? Do you really need to wear those cargo pants with countless pockets? Just what are you expecting to encounter out there that an average golf bag can't accommodate?

That's not to say golf has to be a style-free zone though. Within that simple 'collared shirt and trousers' edict there's enough scope to keep everyone happy thanks to the emergence of 21st-century brands like J Lindeberg, who have been at pains to adhere to golf's dress traditions while taking fabrics, cuts and styling to a younger, sharper level.

So to those who say, 'but I don't want to dress like my old man on the golf course', you don't have to. Imagine your old man in a tight-fitting shirt, a pair of Jesper Parnevik drainpipes and a funky pair of modern golf shoes . . . on second thoughts, don't! It's not a pretty image is it, with the bulges of middle-age spread thrown into the mix. But just as no one would expect him to dress like that, neither do the younger generation have to sport the classic lambswool pullover with M&S slacks look. There's room for everyone, and surely no true golfer really wants to see a steady decline to vest and shellsuit levels?

Off the course, most clubs merely ask you to change if you've got a bit hot and sticky, or look as if you've been dragged through a hedge backwards – which you quite possibly have been in pursuit of your errant ball. Surely that's not too much to ask out of courtesy for others who have to share the bar with you?

Yes, there are some clubs where jacket and tie is still required at certain times or in certain rooms. But you'll almost certainly be aware of such regulations before you join or go and play somewhere, so there's no justification for bemoaning the unfairness of not being able to dress exactly as you please for a couple of fleeting hours. Either don't join or visit such clubs or show a little respect and stick to what is, after all, not too onerous a request. In today's dress-down world you may even find it strangely liberating and good for your self-confidence.

So let's stop whingeing about dress regulations which are, in the overall scheme of things, pretty inconsequential and still broad enough to keep everyone happy. The game will be all the better for not succumbing to our broader society's dress-sense anarchy.

28
METAL SPIKES vs SOFT SPIKES

Metal spikes used to be the only means of achieving decent grip on the course. These days the new king of traction is the lightweight, multi-pronged, plastic soft spike or cleat, promising just as much grip plus a kinder disposition towards feet and turf. But should we be ruing the metal spike's demise or warmly embracing the plastic newcomer?

METAL SPIKES

It is one of the game's saddest laments that the crunching sound of metal spike on asphalt has all but disappeared from the golf clubs of Britain, and sadder still that its successor – the soft spike – goes by

112

the mildly irritating name of cleat in certain quarters. Another of those unwanted Americanisms.

But the metal spike has been swept aside for no good reason and, it would seem, several poor ones. For while the plastic cleat brigade may have enlisted the help of countless 'scientists' to fight their corner, the evidence that either is better for your feet or affords you more grip and traction remains inconclusive to say the least.

The metal spike is still clinging on gamely in certain circles, and its total passing would represent the loss of an institution in the name of alleged progress, much in the same way that Routemaster buses and good old imperial measurements are gradually being bludgeoned out of existence.

But ask yourself this: in slippery, wet, muddy conditions, or when you're perched atop a bank trying to stop yourself toppling forward into the ball, which would you rather rely on to give you the traction you need to execute an effective swing – metal spikes sufficiently long to reassure you that they are indeed penetrating the earth's surface, or plastic, spider-like creations that give so much under your feet you run the risk of looking like Robin Cousins doing the triple salchow at impact?

Then there's the matter of aeration. While many have now convinced themselves that metal spikes damage playing surfaces, some greenkeepers and course managers are lamenting the decrease in natural day-to-day aeration from their tiny puncture marks.

For the final reasons why metal spikes are sorely missed, let's turn to the world of psychology or gamesmanship. Striding loudly across the car park to the 1st tee in metal spikes, chest puffed out and game face on, used to be enough to strike fear into the heart of any slightly jittery opponent already waiting for you there. It's hard to cut quite such an intimidating figure padding your way there inaudibly in soft spikes.

Similarly, spotting an arch rival about to tee off just as you arrive provides the perfect opportunity for some mind games. You strut loudly across the car park, stopping courteously, of course, as he completes his final practice swing. He readies himself for the actual shot and you gingerly, but audibly, sneak a few more paces. He hesitates for a moment, unsure of whether or not you've really stopped. You edge on a little more, and now the damage has been done whether or not you walk any further. Rattled, distracted and half expecting a few more footsteps, he hits a weak shot that promptly hands you a two-shot cushion before you've even hit a ball. Underhand? Perhaps. Good fun? Certainly – but you can't do it in soft spikes.

So for all these reasons, let's hope that metal spikes continue to fight a stern rearguard action, just as those Routemasters and pounds and ounces have been doing, to ensure they never disappear entirely from the fairways of Britain.

SOFT SPIKES

Four hours on a baked links in a pair of metal-spiked shoes can be a crippling experience. The ground is too firm for the spikes to fully penetrate the surface so your weight is supported on 22 little points. By the end of the round you hobble off the course and head straight to the club phonebook to find the number of the nearest chiropodist. It's a scenario that'll never happen if you've moved with the times and changed to soft spikes. You'll cruise around in complete comfort and will feel no urge to change your footwear at the end of the game.

In many cases you won't even need to change your footwear. A number of clubhouses these days are 'soft-spike friendly' so you can finish your round and stroll straight into the bar for a drink and a bite to eat. And it won't just be you who's had an easier time of it; the course will have benefited too.

It's on damp greens where soft spikes really make a difference. In years gone by, if you were a late starter on a drizzly day in the Saturday medal, putting would be a lottery. After 100 gents had stomped around each cup making 22 half-inch-deep holes every step they took, the greens would resemble mini-minefields. As the rules forbid the repair of spike marks, you had to take your chances and hope your ball wouldn't be deflected off-line. But invariably it would be. There are no such problems with soft spikes. Your weight is displaced over a far greater number of points, meaning the greens suffer much less damage. It's courteous to your fellow players to wear soft spikes and, if everyone does, it will mean you take fewer putts – that's surely reason enough to make the switch.

Soft spikes are far more suitable for travelling to watch live golf. Not only do you have the necessary grip to perch on sand dunes and clamber through the rough, but when you decide to rest your legs and find a grandstand, you'll be able to quietly climb the stairs and find a seat. With metal studs you'll sound like you're auditioning for *Billy Elliot* as you clatter about on the steps. Marshals will frantically wave 'Quiet Please' signs at you and you'll feel like a prize turnip as Colin Montgomerie stands away from his putt and directs his steely glare in your direction.

A decent set of soft spikes will be highly durable. You'll find that a single set will last you a full season. The majority of metal spikes are made out of steel that wears down faster than John Daly attempting to run a marathon. Within a couple of months your spikes have become like ball bearings on the bottom of your shoes. You suddenly have less grip than if you had no spikes whatsoever.

Soft spikes are the choice of the conscientious modern golfer who's looking for comfort and flexibility from his golf shoes. Metal spikes are relics of a bygone age: equipment suitable for backward-looking dinosaurs only.

29
SCOTTISH LINKS vs IRISH LINKS

Great Britain and Ireland proudly boast the vast majority of the world's
true links courses, attracting thousands of visitors every year from the
four corners of the earth. Scotland has the heritage and history, while
Ireland has been sneaking up on the rails with stunning newcomers
augmenting an already strong line-up. But which country really does
have the best links?

SCOTTISH LINKS

Ireland is blessed with phenomenal seaside golf courses. From
Royal Portrush in the north to Waterville in the south, from the

European Club in the east to Lahinch in the west, the country is littered with some of the world's most testing and beautiful golfing venues. Rugged and natural, they enchant visitors from all over the globe. It would be slanderous and ignorant to attempt to deny their quality: let's just reflect for a moment on how amazing coastal golf in Ireland is.

Now allow your mind to take a short hop north and east over the Irish Sea. Transport your thoughts to Scotland. Those who've experienced links golf in both countries may need to sit down, as the excitement and fervent anticipation will be causing you to feel faint. For those who've only experienced golf in Ireland it'll be difficult to imagine, but it is true – Scotland's links are superior to those on the Emerald Isle. Offering history, variety and value for money combined with outstanding scenery and clement weather, Scottish links courses are incredible.

Despite what some hopeful Dutchmen may say, the game of golf originated on Scotland's east coast. The history surrounding each of the courses adds considerable extra significance to their appeal. At Montrose, Royal Aberdeen or Gullane it's wonderful to picture famous players of old stalking the fairways. Teeing off at these historic sites sends a shiver down even the most philistine spine.

One of the delightful features of Scotland's links is their variety. Emerging and developing over the past 400 years, each is unique and provides a different challenge. Standing alone is the Old Course at St Andrews. The history and romance of the 'Home of Golf' make it the most exhilarating place to play anywhere in the world. It's beyond compare with any other course and its very existence provides fuel for the argument of the general superiority of Scottish links. Then come the other prestigious Open venues – Turnberry, Carnoustie, Troon and Muirfield. They deliver some of the sternest golfing examinations you're likely to face. These leviathans are backed up by formidable aides-de-camp like Nairn, North Berwick and Western Gailes. There are also hidden gems like Brora, Crail and Machrihanish. They may not be championship venues but they're superb links tracks in the most stunning locations.

Despite the stereotype, the weather in Scotland is pleasant, particularly on the east coast. The influence of the Gulf Stream means it's dry and relatively mild. The links here can be enjoyed all year round. Many of the courses on the west of Ireland (Lahinch as an example) have to close through the winter because the weather is so bad. When squalls come tearing in from the Atlantic it's not a pleasant place to be.

Royal Dornoch in Sutherland is high on the list of the best courses never to hold an Open Championship. Tom Watson described it as 'one of the great courses of the five continents'. In the summer of 2008 you could play this magnificent track for just £82. Old Head of Kinsale in Ireland is also a links of undisputed quality. It may be a spectacular layout but is it fair to ask a green fee of €295 (roughly £235)? Is Old Head three times better than Royal Dornoch? Certainly not.

IRISH LINKS

Some debates in this book present clear-cut opportunities for arguments one way or the other, while others are a little less black and white. The contest between Irish and Scottish links falls very much into the latter category. After all, how could anyone argue against those great Scottish links set in the historic cradle of the game that are undoubtedly among the finest and most well established in the world?

The answer must be by generalisation, for countless individual Irish and Scottish links would buck the arguments that follow. But needs must, so here goes. It is perhaps the phrases 'historic cradle' and 'most well established' that hold the key to the differences, for in some Scottish clubs these sentiments have spurned a greater sense of self-importance than is perhaps good for the comfort of the visiting golfer.

Dour and puritanical would be too strong, but some Scottish links do lean towards an almost perverse pleasure in making the visiting golfer feel a little ill-at-ease or on edge, if for no other reason than that he is simply not well versed in 'their way' of doing things. The assumption can be that 'their way' is indeed '*the* way', and anyone not familiar with 'the way' should be made to feel inferior.

There'll generally be someone on hand to admonish you for taking more than 3 hours to get round – 45 minutes longer than is acceptable – and someone else to annoyingly point out that the 50-mile-an-hour wind which has just wreaked havoc with your scorecard and hair is a mere zephyr.

OK, a touch flippant perhaps, but more pertinently, Scotland's rich golfing heritage does occasionally give its links courses a slightly inflated sense of their own worth – 'our green fee is £120 because we're worth it' as L'Oréal would have it. In Ireland, while green fees can easily match those in Scotland, they often take your money with just the slightest hint of disbelief in their eyes that anyone could really want to pay so much to spend 3 or 4 hours on their particular stretch of golfing turf.

Then there's the world famous 'craic' to factor into the debate. While drink seems to plunge many Scots into a pit of doom and despondency, the very same poison in Ireland seems to generate almost disproportionate conviviality and the most heartfelt of welcomes for even the strangest of golfing strangers.

Finally, while the construction of new links courses has more or less dried up in Scotland, it has carried on apace in Ireland in recent years and will probably continue to do so right up to the time that the conservationists pull the plug once and for all. But don't just take my word for it: set aside a fortnight at the earliest opportunity to take in not only Ireland's classic links like Royal County Down, Royal Portrush and Ballybunion, but also some of the island's most stunning newcomers like Doonbeg, the European Club, Sandy Hills, Tralee, Carne, Connemara and Old Head. It'll set you back a pretty penny but will almost certainly prove to be two of the best weeks of your golfing life.

30
SHORT PUTTS: DEAD WEIGHT vs RAP 'EM IN

Few shots strike more fear into the heart of an average golfer than the 3-foot putt. It should be straightforward but can often seem more intimidating than a 3-iron off the deck from 200 yards. What's the best way to tackle the dreaded short putt? Die the ball into the front of the hole, or bang it into the back of the cup straight and firm?

DEAD WEIGHT

The dead weight putt is golf's very own magic trick that nearly all club golfers would be well advised to take full advantage of. How so? It's the only legal way to effectively widen the hole by just under

1.68 inches. Wouldn't you prefer to be putting to a hole that's just under 6 inches across, rather than the statutory 4¼ inches, as you stand over those nerve-shredding 3-footers you know you simply have to make to keep your score ticking over?

The dead weight putt's remarkable hole-expanding properties are all down to gravity. The golf ball has a diameter of 1.68 inches, so in theory, if 51 per cent of it catches the hole, it will drop. This added tolerance of just under half a ball on either side of the hole increases its effective size by around 25 per cent. If you try to rap 'em in, the hole shrinks back towards its actual size in inverse proportion to a putt's pace, and balls that don't catch enough of the edge will lip out. Even worse, you'll sometimes suffer the dreaded accelerating horseshoe – especially when slopes are involved – perhaps leaving you even further away and opening the door all too readily to the disastrous 'three-putt from nowhere' that converts birdies to bogeys and pars to doubles in the twinkling of an eye.

That is precisely why aggressive short putting is such a bad idea. It reduces the margin for error and has the insidious power to turn opportunity into profligacy.

Yes, you could argue that striking short putts firmly takes any break out of the equation, making every putt nearly straight. But you need steely resolve and a silky smooth action to get away with this. Most of us are blessed with nerves of jelly and a fragile, unreliable stroke. For Tiger, of course, it makes perfect sense to rap 'em in as he makes 95 per cent-plus of all short putts he looks at, so knows that the chances of missing any ultra-rare returns he leaves himself are almost zero. For us, one missed short putt so often leads to another as confidence dissipates and panic sets in. Of course, you'll sometimes overdo it and occasionally dribble one up short, particularly on slower greens. But even if you do, at least it takes the ruinous 'three-putt from nowhere' off the table.

One thing to perhaps be wary of is the slightly crowned hole, which could in theory throw dead weight putts off-line as they die. But even then it's still the better option, as the crown will act as a take-off ramp on firmly struck putts, meaning that even if they do hold their line better, they may not catch enough of the far wall of the cup to proceed downwards.

Overall, there's little doubt that average golfers with inconsistent strokes will not only hole more short ones dead weight, they'll also avert more of those agonising close-range three-putt aberrations. So don't waste energy: give those short ones only what they need to find their way to the bottom of that confidence-boosting, artificially enlarged cup.

RAP 'EM IN

Some mental imagery required. It's the final green in the monthly medal. Your nerves are already in tatters after a day of near disasters and improbable recoveries. You come to the last needing par to make the buffer zone. You find the green in regulation but leave the first uphill putt an agonising 3 feet short. You stand over the par attempt and consider your options – firm and straight or dead weight? Don't be stupid, there's no question over what you should do – rap it in.

Here's the reasoning. Very few golfers relish the prospect of a short putt. Even elite players feel the pressure. The sight of a ball coming to rest 3 feet from the cup triggers sensations similar to those experienced in the dentist's waiting room or just before a job interview. Palms begin to sweat and the stomach tightens, the armies of the dark side of your brain begin construction of a new Death Star with a view to eliminating the last pockets of confident resistance you have.

You must overcome the dark side if you're to have any chance of making this putt. The only way to do this is by being massively positive. What's more positive than going for a firm putt struck with purpose towards the centre of the cup? It's your last and best hope. Believe in your own ability, trust your swing and fire the ball home with authority and conviction. Striking it with pace, you'll have eliminated any subtle breaks on the putt, it will power over any slightly rough terrain and, as the ball will be rolling nicely, it'll grab the hole and practically throw itself down into the cup.

Attempting to dead-weight the putt would merely pander to the dark side. The Emperor and Darth Vader will be laughing all the way to the 19th at just how weak your powers proved to be. You'll make a limp and shaky backswing and feather the putter head through, almost certainly on a different line to that which you intended. The ball will dribble tentatively towards the hole. Travelling at that pathetic speed all manner of outside influences could affect it on its journey. A gust of wind could blow it off-line; the merest of slopes could send the ball sliding past the cup; a grain of sand could deflect it from its path; a worm could suddenly break through the surface of the green and halt the ball's progress; the hole may be slightly crowned and you may not have given it quite enough pace to make it up the crest. The possibilities for disruption are endless.

Trying to cosy a putt into the hole on anything but a silky smooth surface is foolish and highly unpredictable. Rapping it in eliminates all the variables bar one – the quality of your stroke. If you hit the putt well it will go in. Hit it dead weight then you still have to make a good stroke, but you must also judge the slope, the wind and the way the hole is cut. It's simple logic: striking a short putt firmly into the heart of the cup is the most effective and reliable method of holing out.

31

OFF THE BACK PEGS vs OFF THE YELLOWS

Travel to some courses these days and you're presented with a choice on the 1st tee. Do you display your manly bravado and tackle the track at its full yardage, risking a humbling experience, or do you accept your skill level and play the course at a more appropriate length?

OFF THE BACK PEGS

Much like in the earlier chapter where we debated the merits of blades and cavity backs, this comes down to an argument over ambition. Do you strive to move forward and improve your golf or are you content as a mediocre hacker?

If it's the former, you'll understand the importance of pushing yourself, leaving the comfort zone and tackling something a little more difficult. If you fall into the latter camp, that's a shame. Maybe these words will convince you to change your laissez-faire attitude.

Let's get one thing straight: your score will always be higher from the back tees. It's simple logic. But have a close look at the scorecard before you tee off. You'll probably find the par and the standard scratch score (SSS) are higher from the back pegs as well. There are many courses where a long par 4 from the yellows is stretched by 20 yards for the back tees to become a relatively straightforward par 5. Your total score may be higher, but in relation to SSS you might even fare a little better.

Yes, the holes will look more intimidating and your confidence might take a bashing at first. But by pushing yourself you'll improve. If you take on someone better than you at tennis you'll raise your game and play better shots. Play a tough course from the back pegs and you'll be forced to hit longer, straighter drives and solid long-iron approaches. It's good for your game.

Going to a prestigious course and playing from the 'tiger tees' is like going to a ski resort and tackling the toughest black run on the mountain. Even if you don't get down it with much grace or style, you'll still have done it. Think of the feeling of accomplishment when you reach the bottom/18th green and look back at the slope/course. The glühwein in the mountain restaurant or the pint in the clubhouse tastes that bit better when you feel like you've achieved something.

Many people will say, 'But I just play golf for fun.' If you play golf purely for fun then it shouldn't matter what tees you hit off. Try going off the backs. Imagine the fun you'll have as you negotiate the full length of a layout, visiting sections of the course you didn't even know existed. If you're a fun-seeker playing with someone who takes the sport seriously then you owe it to them to take on the course from the backs.

If you play from the forward tees you often get a false impression of a layout. Bunkers and other hazards are taken out of the equation and par 4s can be reached with a drive and a flick, rather than two full shots. If you're lucky enough to play a top course that's visited by a professional tour, you simply have to play it as the pros would (if it's allowed). It gives you an understanding of the difficulty levels facing the top players, so when you next see them negotiating the track in five under par, your appreciation and enjoyment will reach new levels.

The choice is clear: approach every course with determination and ambition. Play from the back pegs.

OFF THE YELLOWS

What constitutes a tough test in terms of length? For a tour pro it might now be 7,000-plus yards, but for most average golfers, the yellow tees – typically 5,800 to 6,300 yards – still pose a stern enough examination, because for them, length isn't the sole challenge. The problem with the back pegs is that, although they may at first have some novelty value, it isn't long before the joke wears off and it just becomes one long, dispiriting slog.

Conversely, everyone can enjoy themselves off the yellows because everyone can at least get round without having to whip the head cover off for every approach. Golf's length benchmark may have changed with the advent of the modern 'championship' layout, but few of us are complaining that our courses are too short to test us even off the yellows. For even though we're nearly all hitting it further than ever, every time we set foot on the course there are countless things beyond mere length that stand between us and success – short-game prowess, accurate iron play and a deft putting touch, for example. To reduce the game's challenge to length alone by always heading off to the back tees turns a multidimensional game into a one-dimensional one – an argument put forward with increasing persistence by those who reside closer to the bottom of the tour driving distance stats than the top.

Golf clubs need to attract repeat business and retain members. This is why many insist on all non-competition play being from the yellows. They know that given the choice many golfers would be tempted to play off the backs, biting off more than their games can chew and potentially shooting hundreds. This will leave them with less than fond memories, and less enthusiasm to return: 'We're not going back there – worst score I shot all year.' Not what golf clubs want at all.

At some clubs – especially newer ones – you will be given free rein to play off whatever tees you like, and there will always be some misguided fool who persuades you it'll be a real hoot to play off the blacks, golds or whatever colour stands for impossible at this particular track. And it may well be a hoot for four holes until your party has racked up a hatful of doubles, trebles and 'others', while failing to reach a single green in regulation. As you leave the 4th green, someone else has the merciful wisdom to call an emergency summit, at which point common sense prevails and you revert to the yellows, increasing your enjoyment factor exponentially from there on in.

You see, those back pegs weren't designed for the typical golfer – they were put in for long-hitting pros and amateurs for whom, given the extra distance they hit it, they provide a similar challenge to the one average handicappers face off the yellows. So stick to your level; don't try and play a game with which you are unfamiliar, and only venture off the backs when you have no choice in the matter. It's much more likely to keep you coming back for more.

32
CLUBHOUSE PRE-ROUND OR POST-ROUND

When is the best time to sit down and experience the clubhouse environment? Before the round when hopes are high and your mood buoyant with anticipation, or after battle when you are mentally and physically exhausted and in need of some restorative sustenance?

PRE-ROUND

In an ideal world, you'd get to the course well ahead of your tee-time, meet, greet and share a coffee or two with your mates, play your game and then retire to the bar for drinks and a bite to eat as you dissect the round and put the world to rights afterwards.

Sadly, that ideal scenario is rarely possible in our busy modern lives. When we put the kids and the other half in the mix, along with all those little jobs around the house that we know – or have been told – need our urgent attention, how many of us can really spare the full 6 or 7 hours for that perfect golfing day very often? So do you opt for the clubhouse before or after your round? It has to be before for a number of reasons.

First, ahead of the game you can plan things precisely because you know when you're teeing off. If you go for the post-round drinks option knowing you have to be home by a certain time, you'll end up feeling rushed and pressured if things take longer than anticipated, and that will probably be reflected in your score.

Pre-round, you can meet an hour before the off, catch up with the news over a civilised cup of coffee and a sumptuously filled bacon butty, or perhaps even indulge craftily in the full fry-up that has long since been scribbled off the home dining menu by those concerned about your long-term survival.

More importantly, it's here where the scene and any appropriate bets for the round ahead are set. The conversation flows freely: 'Dave's playing steadily so I'd expect him to be round about his handicap. Jim's definitely due for a low one – could be today. Not sure if Frank's going to be up to much today after than nasty bout of the Shermans last week.' Everyone talks themselves either up or down accordingly and an appropriate deal is struck. What 'bits' are you playing for – birdies, sand saves, nearest the pins, longest drives?

Doing all this over a leisurely pre-round snack means you'll arrive at the 1st tee relaxed yet geed up and ready to go. Far better than rushing to the tee, playing off, then trying to negotiate the bets with you in the centre of the fairway, and Dave scything around in the undergrowth like the Grim Reaper on a particularly busy morning.

Doing the social bit pre-round also avoids that awkward scenario where Jim has played like a drain, not spoken to anyone for the last six holes, yet still feels obliged to stay for a drink. He sits staring vacantly into his beer, killing both mood and conversation. You can't properly celebrate your win, and he's too sensitive for any teasing.

No – pre-round is the way to go. Bacon butties, coffee and chit-chat work best before the round while everyone's still in the mood, rather than afterwards when one of you quite possibly won't be. So be sociable – play your round, settle up any debts, sort out next week's game and go home.

POST-ROUND

You've just lost another ball on the 13th. Your score is so far above handicap even level eagles wouldn't get you back to buffer. There's little to keep you in a positive frame of mind. Don't worry, there's still one element of the day to look forward to – a refreshing pint of your favourite ale back in the clubhouse. Suddenly everything looks a little rosier and those last few holes are less of a struggle. Thank God for the 19th.

Whether you've had a good or a bad round, there's nothing to beat a bit of post-round banter in the clubhouse. When you've recorded a good score you can revel in recounting your exploits and achievements. If you've had a shocker you can elicit bursts of rapturous laughter as you describe exactly how your ball finished up a tree on the 8th or how you racked up a nine at the par 3 12th. The best thing is that, no matter how poorly you've played, there'll always be someone in the bar who has fared worse. The ideal scenario is that you're taking taxis or are within walking distance of home so you can turn the post-round debriefing into a little more of a party. There's no better way to reinstil confidence in your game than with the aid of a few drinks.

If you go straight home after a bad round you'll be depressed and full of pent-up frustration. Saunter in for a drink and laugh it off with your friends and you'll go home in an altogether better frame of mind. You owe it to your family to spend an hour or so chilling out in the bar. Take off your sweaty golf clothes and enjoy a rejuvenating shower, put on a clean shirt and pair of trousers and head in. Relax in a comfy chair and begin to let the golf ebb away from your mind. Ahhh, lovely.

On a hot summer's day when the round has taken 5 hours, how good the first sip of a pint tastes. It'll be particularly enjoyable if the club has a verandah or outside area from where you can watch other golfers finishing. There's nothing better than watching your pals make a right royal hash of the last from the safety of the clubhouse with a drink in your hand.

A bacon roll and coffee before your game is certainly a pleasant way to start the day, but you can never really relax pre-round. You're too psyched up to go out and play to really enjoy the leather armchairs or to take a little time to peruse the competition boards on the walls. After a round you're in pure wind-down mode. Your work for the day is done (good or bad) and you can just enjoy your surroundings and some excellent company. Laugh about the good luck and bad luck you experienced. Toast the day's winners and commiserate with those who didn't perform quite so well. The 19th is the best hole on the course.

33

TRADITION vs TECHNOLOGY

The sport of golf is over 500 years old and in that time the technology of the game has evolved dramatically. Also in that time, however, a huge amount of golfing tradition has developed. Both progress and heritage are core to our great game but can they co-exist? And, if one had to go, which should it be?

TRADITION

Golf's great heritage and its many traditions are what make it such a unique and beloved sport. It's sad that technological advances threaten the very heart of the game.

Equipment has evolved to a point where the poorer player is given unreasonable levels of assistance, and the advantages previously enjoyed by the precise ball-striker are greatly diminished. The use of electric trolleys by all-and-sundry eliminates some of the physical demands of the game, while distance-measuring devices have removed the requirement for skill and judgement. On a more aesthetic level, modern golf attire is vulgar and looks more like something in which you'd see an Olympic athlete warming up than an elegant golfer striding the fairways.

Advocating tradition in golf is not to be in favour of things that are aged or outdated. Luke Donald has a traditional golf swing but neither he nor it is old. *Mizuno* makes sleek and classically-styled irons but the ones you see on the shelves of your pro shop are straight off today's production line.

Luke Donald's swing is good because it's traditional; *Mizuno*'s bladed irons have become 'traditional' because they're so good.

It is, however, with equipment that technological advances have been most detrimental to golf. The latest balls and oversized drivers allow players with poor and inconsistent swings to hit the ball longer and straighter than they should be able to; utility clubs negate the need to hit a long iron (a previous indicator of a good golfer); huge cavity-back irons forgive an embarrassment of faults, while belly and broom-handle putters give those with even the most twitchy strokes a chance on the greens.

Technology conceals faults in a struggling player's game. For those looking to improve, this is not helpful. The results may be acceptable but the method is not and it's liable to break down more fully at any moment.

There are other technological advances that have gone too far towards levelling the playing field in golf – the range finder or GPS system for instance. In days gone by, the ability to judge distance was a crucial golfing skill. Yes, you may have had guidance from a yardage book, but you'd still have to calculate, or estimate, the exact distance. Now, with a distance-measuring device, you know precisely how far you have from wherever you are, even if you're on the wrong fairway. It's basically cheating.

When it comes to clothing, sporting technology has arrived at the expense of style. Sports manufacturers have entered the golf clothing market and have brought with them designs that wouldn't be out of place in the *Tour de France*. The 'moisture-wicking' fabrics may be cooling but they're certainly not cool.

Then look at golf shoes. Many modern designs are horrendous – more like running trainers or football boots than golf shoes. Surely anyone with even a hint of style would feel more at ease in a pair of smart *Footjoy Classics?*

Technology is menacing our game on all sides. Shorter courses are becoming obsolete because of distance-maximising equipment, belly putters and range finders are removing the requirement for skill and the game is an increasingly style-free zone. It's got to stop.

TECHNOLOGY

Step back a moment to the 1970s, and imagine Raymond Baxter's rich fruity tones on *Tomorrow's World* emanating from the black and white TV in the corner of the lounge: '. . . and thirty years from now, golfers will be using drivers the size of frying pans and putters that look like the Starship Enterprise.' We'd have looked at him with the same incredulity as if he'd just told us one day we'd be carrying round personal phones to keep us all in constant contact, or that surgeons would be able to operate without the need of a scalpel.

Just as in all aspects of life, and much though the naysayers may deny it, technological progress in golf has made the game easier and more enjoyable for all.

Tradition, of course, has an admirable place in our history books. But when we look fondly back and marvel at how Bobby Jones or Ben Hogan shot *those* scores using *that* equipment on *those* greens, it doesn't mean we hanker after the same on the fairways of the 21st century. Just as no laptop user would ever want to revert to typewriter and manual filing, no sane golfer would ever want to give up the game's many technological advances.

Debates over blades versus cavity backs and long irons versus utility clubs are covered elsewhere in this book, where hopefully you'll have found yourself nodding vigorously in agreement with the respective arguments for progress. But drivers and putters are perhaps even more clear-cut cases. Only the very best ball-strikers could coax anything out of those old small-headed wooden drivers. For the rest, every drive was a battle with uncertainty. Other than on those rare occasions when we got it right out of the pin-headed sweetspot, what kind of flight and shape could we expect? Often, we snookered ourselves insurmountably at the start of every hole. Now, 460cc monster titanium heads in a range of radical shapes have transformed the big stick into the easiest club of all – tee it high and whack it away. And at the far end of the hole, huge mallets are on hand to iron out some of the wobbles in our putting strokes, leaving us plucking the ball out of the hole more often than with those slender blades of old.

We have electric trolleys to ease the weight burden; we have outerwear that is light and indeed waterproof rather than cumbersome and sponge-like in anything more than a shower; we have GPS devices to tell us exactly where we are on a hole so we're not left staring nonplussed at a yardage book trying to work out if we're by that bush or that mound; and we have costly premium balls that aren't rendered unusable by the first random strike of the day.

Driving a vintage car must certainly be a wonderful experience, but is that car better-equipped to cope with the demands of today's busy highways than even the most basic modern family saloon? Definitely not, and it's the same with golf. Tradition demands our respect and attracts our historical curiosity, but we wouldn't want to live with it day to day.

34

FOUR-BALL vs FOURSOMES

Golf is a sociable sport, but generally it's an individual one. In four-ball and foursomes you have a partner to help or hinder. Four-ball events see you both playing your own balls with the better score counting; in foursomes you play alternate shots. Which is golf's top pairs format?

FOUR-BALL

Golf is an individual sport. When you put together a good score, achieve a handicap cut or fire a hole-in-one it's down to one person – you. If you have a bad day there's nobody else to blame and you're forced to examine the reasons for the poor performance. It's one of the principal reasons why golf is such an addictive sport. Four-ball better-ball is a fun extension of the individual game. It allows you to enjoy playing in a team while remaining in control of your own destiny. Foursomes is an unpleasant corruption of golf. You walk the whole course but don't get to play all the shots and are forced to rely on another player. It's a format to be avoided at all costs.

Foursomes can only really be enjoyed when both you and your partner are playing well. When you're on form and he's having an off day, 3 hours in a dentist's chair would be preferable to 3 hours on the links. It goes something like this: you fire one majestically down the centre of the fairway; he shanks one out of bounds. You knock one confidently on to the centre of the green; he putts into a bunker. You splash out to 2 feet; he misses the putt. 'I won't say sorry,' he says. *You bloody well should*, you think. On the other side of the coin, it's even more cringingly awful when you're having a disaster and your partner is playing well. You just don't know where to look as you slice one into the trees or double-hit a chip. If it were just your problem you could NR with dignity and live to fight another day. As it's foursomes you've got to keep battling to the bitter end.

Golf's darkest outer limits can be observed when both foursomes partners are playing badly. One bad shot begets another and you pull each other down into the seventh level of golfing hell. Neither of you will want to step on a golf course for weeks afterwards.

In four-ball it doesn't matter when one player is firing on all cylinders and the other is struggling. The form horse can carry his ailing partner. The former receives the plaudits and eternal gratitude from the latter while the duffer has a chance to experience victory even when playing poorly. Even better, he can still contribute. He might not be able to hit his hat for 17 holes, but on the 18th he may pitch in or hole a crucial putt. Even when both players are performing below their best they could still scrape a win. If they 'dovetail' or 'ham and egg' effectively they could still time it so they don't have their worst holes concurrently. It's like playing your individual game with a back-up. How we'd all like that in the Saturday medal. So next time someone asks you to make up a four, be sure to politely enquire what format they're playing. If the answer's foursomes think fast and come up with a good excuse for non-attendance.

FOURSOMES

The reason why the alternate-shot format of foursomes surpasses four-ball better-ball is that you're inescapably in it together for the duration – for better, for worse, for richer, for poorer, in sickness and in health. Both players are always part of the action whether in the middle of the fairway discussing what club they need for the next shot, or doing passable impressions of David Bellamy as they try to formulate an effective escape plan from the patch of lush vegetation where their ball lies.

In four-ball, if it all goes horribly wrong for you off the tee, the most valuable contribution you'll make for the next 15 minutes will be tending the flag for everyone else when they reach the green, having walked miserably down the side of the fairway feeling glum, useless and detached. If you're having a particularly horrid day, the above scenario will be repeated ad infinitum and you'll end up little more than a spectator while all the others are enjoying themselves. Where's the fun in that – and indeed any sense of real satisfaction, even if your partner miraculously carries the team single-handedly to victory?

The couple that truly plays the better golf will always emerge victorious in foursomes because there's simply no hiding-place. In four-ball, if one of you is playing a blinder and the other is having a howler, you might still run out the winners over a pair who have both played pretty steady golf – somehow that just doesn't seem fair.

In foursomes you'll be working as a team even when one puts the other in trouble. Mirroring life itself, it's when you muck in together rather than going it alone that you often make the best of a bad situation. Good foursomes players stick together through thick and thin – much like a good marriage; and they master the art of never saying sorry – less like a good marriage!

In foursomes you'll be talking to each other the whole time, cajoling, encouraging and discussing the best options for the shot or hole ahead. There's no concept of 'my ball', only 'our ball'. In four-ball, however much you try to convince yourself that you're playing as a team, the concept of 'my ball' still exists to a much greater degree, hence the common phrases 'At least *my* ball's still in play' or 'Good job *I* came in there with you in trouble'.

And if you really get a taste for the alternate-shot format and venture into the much-derided world of mixed foursomes, you'll get to experience an entirely different game, playing from places you've never before been, and discovering parts of the course you never even knew existed. It gives you a better perspective on the game that others play.

Foursomes is superior to four-ball because it's a much tougher test, and the pair that plays the better golf together will always come out on top. That isn't always the case in four-ball. The concepts of 'we', 'our' and 'us' are what make foursomes the great team game; four-ball allows too much scope for 'I', 'mine' and 'me'.

35

JACK NICKLAUS vs
JAMES BRAID

*Nicklaus and Braid were among the finest players of their respective
generations, with a host of major titles to their names. However, this
debate is not concerned with their playing careers, but rather the course
design work to which both turned in earnest. The question is, simply,
who is the better champion golfer turned course architect?*

JACK NICKLAUS

Choosing between Nicklaus and Braid as designers is a tricky one
for many reasons, not least that personal tastes vary greatly, and that
the two worked in different eras with different resources and means
at their disposal.

Without going into the finer elements of each man's design traits – for example, Braid's reliance on slightly raised greens and subtle bunkering; Nicklaus's more liberal use of sand and dog-legs (though Braid is often said to have 'invented' the latter) – it is an indisputable fact that the latest CAD technology and earth-moving potential has allowed Nicklaus to make the very best use of any land offered to him. Braid was largely restricted to following whatever routing the terrain seemed to naturally suggest, with his major input revolving around the design and location of greens and hazards. So Nicklaus has been able to shape things much more to his or his clients' precise needs, building structured courses in which he can control the ebb and flow of difficulty and breathing space at will.

Nicklaus layouts are, of course, bang up to date too, while many of Braid's have fallen behind advances in equipment technology, rendering certain hazards obsolete and in need of relocation. Nicklaus courses are more than capable of challenging the game's elite, as evidenced by the fact that around a third have gone on to stage top professional or amateur events, including majors and the Ryder Cup. Braid's courses have largely fallen from the tour schedules, with the exception of Carnoustie – but his input there was as remodeller in 1926 rather than original creator. Perhaps nowhere is the power shift more evident that at Gleneagles, where Braid's King's Course – perhaps his finest work – has been knocked off the top perch by Nicklaus's PGA Centenary, the Scottish resort's new tour venue and host course for the 2014 Ryder Cup.

That reference to Carnoustie brings us neatly to another point of difference. While virtually all Nicklaus's work is original design (300 or so completed courses with 100 more under construction), many of the 200 or so courses associated with Braid involved remodelling work rather than initial creation, especially famous links like Troon, Ballybunion and Prestwick. So Nicklaus is by far the more prolific designer.

More global too, for while Braid's motion sickness and fear of flying had him firmly confined within these shores, Nicklaus's design CV reads like the script for a Judith Chalmers travel series – China, Brunei, New Zealand, Indonesia, Dominican Republic and Tahiti to name but a few. Private jets and the wonders of modern travel have certainly helped, but even so, it is Nicklaus who will leave the more far-reaching legacy for generations to come than the less adventurous Braid.

Although Braid's work is far more evident than Nicklaus's in Great Britain and Ireland, the handful of projects that Nicklaus has undertaken here have almost invariably found their way on to tour schedules, often the flagship European Tour – Hanbury Manor, St Mellion, the London Club, Gleneagles PGA Centenary and Mount Juliet, for example.

Braid was probably the best player-turned-designer of his time; Nicklaus the best of our time. But when you put it all together, you would have to say that Nicklaus is the best of all time . . . at least, that is, until Tiger really gets stuck into course design.

JAMES BRAID

There can be no denying that Jack Nicklaus is a prolific and clever golf course architect. His layouts are highly respected and a number are regularly used for significant professional tournaments. It's for this reason as much as for his name that the Golden Bear can command a handsome fee for his involvement in a project. Jack is a superb designer and it would be incorrect to try and discredit him.

Let's then concentrate on Braid, his masterpieces and what makes them so fabulous. Born in Earlsferry, Fife, in 1870, Braid grew up playing golf on the links at Elie. He turned professional in 1896 and in 1901 won his first Open Championship; he had four more to his name by 1910. Braid became club pro at Walton Heath in 1903, where he remained until his death in 1950. His golfing credentials were second to none.

By the time of his death Braid was, however, perhaps as well known for his golf course architecture as for his exploits as a player. From Brora in the north to St Enodoc in the south, the Scot was responsible for, or had contributed to, the design of over 200 courses throughout the British Isles. Many of his creations continue to appear in the upper echelons of course ranking lists year after year. Let's consider a couple of the best:

- The King's Course at Gleneagles is perhaps Braid's most famous creation. A heathland track set high in the hilly heartland of Perthshire, it rises and falls as it coils its way past pines and heather over springy moorland turf. As with all Braid courses, every hole is unique and memorable. From the driveable par 4 14th to the testing 17th, your shot-making skills will be tested to their limits.
- In 1907 Braid travelled to Cornwall where he laid out an 18-hole course at St Enodoc, now known as the Church Course. Despite some alterations to the layout over the years, golfers still play the course essentially as Braid designed it. It's an exhilarating and refreshing links, unlike any other you'll play. Braid made use of the huge dunes to create an undulating track where you'll encounter all manner of lies and stances and must have a superb imagination to get round in a sensible score.

Something notable through all of Braid's work was his use of natural terrain and contours. Working in an age before massive earth-moving was an option, Braid managed to create holes with dramatic slopes and undulations simply by allowing holes to run along the lie of the land. His choice of green sites was particularly impressive as he often decided to build putting surfaces into slopes, thereby creating distinctive and testing green complexes. As a successful professional golfer, Braid understood exactly what made a golf hole challenging. His clever use of bunkering was evidence of this and the strategic placement of sand was a feature on all his courses.

James Braid was a visionary and the fact that so many of his courses have stood the test of time is proof of his great skill as a course designer.

36

THE MASTERS vs THE OPEN

Debate on the best tournament in world golf usually comes down to a straight choice between The Masters, played every April among the resplendent azaleas of Augusta National in Georgia, USA, and The Open, played every July over one of the nine rugged links courses on the current championship rota.

THE MASTERS

A Sunday evening in mid March; not even the *Antiques Roadshow* can distract you from the inexorable feeling winter will never end. Michael Aspel signs off and your eyelids begin to droop. But then through a sleepy haze you spy a collage of greens and pinks before the familiar sound of metal on surlyn wakes you with an adrenalin-fuelled jolt. Can it be? Yes, thank God, it's just two weeks until The Masters. The pulse starts racing, the clubs are reclaimed from the cupboard under the stairs, golf shoes are buffed and the flat cap located. The Masters heralds the start of a new golf season. Like the first daffodil or first returning swallow, its coming generates feelings of hope and promise in every golfer. No other event inspires more people to get out on to the fairways.

The avid golf fan knows every square foot of Augusta. They've watched countless Masters and can recognise each hole from the most fleeting glimpse. It's fantastic television because you know exactly what the player is facing. You know they must hit a draw from the 13th tee, and if a ball starts to roll off the front of the 15th green, nothing will stop it reaching the water. Who among us could describe the 4th at Royal Troon or the view from the 10th tee at Royal Lytham? Not many.

Augusta represents the pinnacle of course preparation and pre-sentation. The greens are smooth silk, none in the world run truer; the fairways are like a giant velvet spring-loaded carpet, not a blade of grass is out of place. The Masters is a showcase of greenkeeping excellence, a demonstration of how a course can be maintained. Just compare it with the dusty moonscape that was Hoylake in 2006. The viewing public could actually watch the grass on the greens dying over the four days. In comparison to Augusta, The Open venues are presented about as well as a council-run pitch and putt in mid October.

Advances in technology mean the vast majority of today's professionals can drive the ball 300 yards and fire lofted approaches into greens 240 yards distant. The purest ball strikers have lost their advantage so the best players are now determined by their skills on and around the greens. The Masters is the greatest competition on planet golf because it provides the ultimate short-game test and therefore identifies the best golfers. The winner will be a magician from within 50 yards of the flag. He'll have a complete arsenal of chips, pitches and flops and his putting will be rock solid. The Open doesn't demand such incredible levels of imagination. Master the chip and run and it's game on. It means there's little to separate the field and this is why it has recently thrown up obscure champions like Paul Lawrie, Ben Curtis and Todd Hamilton. The Masters will never be won by a golfing nobody because it's simply too difficult. The day Todd Hamilton wins The Masters I'll eat his rescue club.

THE OPEN

Perhaps the key argument for superiority between The Open and The Masters revolves around whether you prefer your golf 'au naturel', unfettered by elaborate visual decoration, or artificially enhanced in a way only the Americans can, where what you see – beautiful though it may be – is at least partly the result of some judicious cosmetic tweaking.

The Masters is certainly a thrilling golfing spectacle that awakens the British golfing public from enforced hibernation every April, with its spectacular colours and immaculately presented fairways providing the catalyst to resume weather-restricted playing schedules. At Augusta National not only is there not a blade of grass out of place, but also the bare patches are even tinted green where not a blade exists. Rumour has it even the blueness of the ponds may be more to do with man than nature. But should a golf course really go to such lengths, or is that taking things too far in a sport that was originally played where nature seemed to invite, often by the sea?

It's just such natural seaside environments that the R&A presents to the world's best every July at The Open, nowhere more so than at Hoylake in 2006. The dusty, arid landscape there may have had the country club set choking on their club sandwiches and fries, but there was no trickery at work here. The course was simply a product of that summer's exceptionally hot, dry spell, and rather than pumping countless gallons of precious water on to fairways to green things up, the R&A simply let nature more or less dictate the playing conditions. The Green Jackets at Augusta probably thought they'd mistakenly tuned in to a live lunar broadcast – but it was simply golf at its unadulterated best.

Of course if you want to reinforce The Open's status as golf's premier event, there's the small matter of 74 years' more history to take into consideration, with the original 'Belt' first being played for at Prestwick in 1860. Bobby Jones's first Masters invites didn't drop on to his chums' doormats until 1934.

And The Open is still an 'open' event too, in which any club pro or top amateur has a chance – albeit a remote one – of taking his place in the field come Thursday of Open week. True, he must first negotiate qualifying events where there's fierce competition for just a handful of places, but at Augusta he'd face just as stern a test in simply laying his hands on one of the ultra-scarce admission tickets.

And one final point. If you want to watch The Open live, you can just turn up – even if tickets are now a little on the pricey side. If you want to watch The Masters live, you can't – unless you're one of the privileged few. Until a few short years ago, the Augusta folk deemed their course so sacred that they wouldn't even allow live TV coverage of the front nine, only the back nine. On Open Thursday and Friday the BBC will happily beam live pictures into your living room from dawn till dusk, with true obsessives only needing to drag themselves away for those unavoidable calls of nature.

The Open is the greatest golf tournament in the world because it is just that – open and accessible to many more than The Masters.

37

CONSISTENCY vs SCRAMBLING

For some golfers nothing is more satisfying than a steady and competent round with no mistakes. Others get maximum enjoyment from a flair-filled roller-coaster round featuring double bogeys and chip-in birdies, out of bounds and up-and-downs. Which camp do you fall into?

CONSISTENCY

Who wants to be spasmodically good at something? It's stressful and frustrating to have to battle through to complete a task. Would you like to be periodically good at driving a car? Imagine that on 50 per cent of journeys you had to fight really hard not to leave the road or crash into someone in the car park at Tesco.

Here are two post-round scenarios. Consider which you would find more satisfying:

- You walk off the 18th green having played solidly. You've hardly made a mistake. You'd formulated a plan for the game and done your best to stick to it, hitting fairways and greens and making use of your shot holes. You feel you've completed your objective and thoroughly deserve a well-earned pint.
- You walk off the 18th in a muck sweat, having endured a stressful and seemingly never-ending ordeal. Somehow you've managed to make it home in the buffer zone but you nearly suffered a heart attack in the process. You've had a lucky ricochet from a tree, a chip-in for a bogey and you've holed countless putts that on other days just wouldn't have dropped. You're looking forward to a stiff drink but it will be restorative rather than celebratory.

Everyone aspires to be consistent at golf. Even the most swash-buckling stars like Seve or Arnie were endeavouring to get the ball on fairways and greens. Those who say they prefer to be on the back foot, always being forced to get up and down or make saving putts, are delusional.

If you're consistently hitting fairways and greens you're playing good golf. You should be scoring well. If not, it might just require a little tweak to your putting stroke in order to light the spark and really find some low numbers. If you're having to scramble to make pars, even if you're good at doing it, you're not going to improve without a dramatic swing change or some other significant altera-tion. How can you be happy with that situation?

Let's examine two of Tiger Woods' major victories. At Hoylake in 2006 he carefully plotted his way round the links in a superbly measured masterclass of long iron play and lag putting. His consistent approach meant he eclipsed his rivals and won with ease. At the 2005 Masters Tiger was not on form. He was swinging the club flat and his driving was wild. Despite this, he somehow managed to scramble his way to victory, holing countless yards of putts and that ludicrous chip at the 16th. It may have been entertaining but it didn't compare to Hoylake as a display of golfing prowess.

Consider finally another major – Nick Faldo's 18 straight pars to win the 1987 Open at a fog-bound Muirfield. It was one of the most impressive examples of control and patience ever seen on a golf course, a remarkable and admirable victory epitomising golfing consistency. Who can say they wouldn't be happy walking off their home course having recorded 18 pars?

SCRAMBLING

Once it has finally dawned on you that total mastery of the long game and full swing is likely to remain for ever beyond your reach, what else is there to look forward to on your lifelong journey of golfing discovery? How else can you possibly break free from the shackles of a prematurely stagnant handicap and send your scores tumbling once more?

Improved form with the putter, perhaps. But if you're among the golfing majority whose games reside at the opposite end of the scale to the one marked 'consistency', improving your scrambling skills first would then leave you putting – or perhaps even tapping in – for par more often than bogey.

Learning how to squeeze every last drop out of a round is fun. If you get good at it and really embrace the scrambler's mindset, you'll find that rather than cursing every missed green you'll be trotting merrily up the fairway after your disobedient ball with a spring in your step, rejoicing at another opportunity to show off your short-game virtuosity – and potentially irritate the hell out of your opponent. Every greenside salvage operation you face is a unique challenge to be relished, though you must set realistic goals as to what constitutes a good result from where your wayward ball has taken you this time. Coaxing it close from a bare lie over a bunker to a rock-hard putting surface sloping away from you may not be realistic. Simply keeping it on the green could be.

Of course you'll need to spend time learning all the shots you're likely to need from the myriad tricky spots and lies you leave yourself. But regardless of whether or not you practise specifically, your very inconsistency will count in your favour as you'll have given yourself plenty of learning experience on the course itself over the years. Mr 'Fairways and Greens', meanwhile, may not be quite so skilled in the art of scrambling – he's not had as much chance as you to learn, as he misses so few greens and consequently has never really seen the point in wasting precious practice time working at something he rarely needs. So when he does finally need it, he may not have a clue how to play the shot required. You – the master scrambler – most assuredly will.

Competent scrambling can have a beneficial knock-on effect on your approach play too. The knowledge that you don't necessarily have to hit the green to make par can free you up to play more positively and less cautiously, resulting – somewhat ironically – in potentially more consistent results.

And if you become a truly skilled scrambler you'll quickly develop a reputation as someone to be avoided at all costs in the club knockout. After all, getting up and down from all over the park can be debilitatingly demoralising for any opponent – especially Mr Consistent!

38
SENIORS' TOURS vs WOMEN'S TOURS

For most golf fans, the main PGA and European tours are where it's at. But what about the seniors and the women? Their schedules also attract plenty of TV coverage, especially in the States. If you had to choose between the 50-plus brigade whose golf games you perhaps grew up with, or the best women players on the planet, who would you rather watch?

SENIORS' TOURS

While women rightly take their games every bit as seriously as men in their quest to climb the rankings, seniors' golf is much more about good old-fashioned fun. Admittedly, some approach the 'round bellies' tour, as Lee Trevino christened it, with as much determination and commitment as they did the regular tour – not surprising given the riches on offer, especially in the States. But far more are so chuffed at the new lease of golfing life their 50th birthday brings, it shines through in the way they happily go about their business. After perhaps five years of main tour struggles, they're eternally grateful for the chance to win good money once more, long after their games were last competitive in an absolute sense.

So they walk around with smiles on their faces, chatting to each other, the crowds and anyone else who'll listen, and giving the impression they're doing what you're supposed to on the golf course – enjoying themselves.

As for those round bellies, don't be deceived – they can still play a bit too, even if the term 'athletic build' no longer applies. And they're not all like that anyway. Among the recent 50-turners is a new breed of 'super-senior', still every bit as physically fit as his younger counterpart – think Bernhard Langer, Nick Faldo and Greg Norman. Along with others like Jay Haas and Fred Funk, they've all shown they're still more than capable of a decent finish or two on the main tour.

The seniors' tours rekindle old rivalries for players and spectators too. Add European legends Sandy Lyle and Ian Woosnam to the mix – both of whom have now also started their senior careers – and many 40- and 50-somethings will go nostalgically misty-eyed as they recall the magnificent shoot-outs these heroes treated them to in the 1980s and 1990s, while eagerly anticipating battles rejoined. For others it has perhaps been Palmer, Nicklaus, Trevino and Watson who have made seniors' golf such a watchable spectacle in recent decades.

Above all, the seniors are a source of inspiration to us all as the years roll by. You'll see a wide range of quirky and jerky swings on display which are still highly effective despite backs, shoulders, knees and other joints that have seized up or gone under the career-saving knife. It's a source of unending wonder that some can get it round at all. But get it round they do, giving us all fresh hope that the dreaded 'five-oh' need not be the end of our golf as we know it, however much our bodies decline to do what they once did, and flex where they once flexed.

Finally, there are others, like Tom Watson, who inspire for the very opposite reason. His timeless swing remains virtually indistinguishable from the one he used to amass all those majors in the 1970s and 1980s, so much so that it leaves you scratching your head that he isn't still winning on the main tour.

The ladies are certainly not without their merits, but seniors' golf has the edge for reasons of nostalgia, inspiration and enjoyment.

WOMEN'S TOURS

A group of elite professionals at the pinnacle of their sport, in their physical prime and producing the best golf of their lives, versus a bunch of ageing has-beens desperately clinging to past glories as their skills fade. That's what the choice between watching women's or seniors' golf boils down to.

Women's professional golf is exciting and of an ever-increasing quality. The tournaments are highly competitive and star names like Lorena Ochoa, Paula Creamer and Michelle Wie are attracting more and more young women to the game. The seniors may deliver the odd thrilling moment, inspiring memories of bygone days, but their best performances are behind them and they won't now be encouraging many youngsters to pick up a club.

This century, two women have raised the profile of women's golf through their phenomenal performances on the course:

- Annika Sorenstam retired at the end of 2008 as the most successful female golfer of the modern era. She won over 90 professional tournaments around the world and picked up 10 major titles. In 2001 she became the first female golfer to score a 59 in competitive play – a feat not yet achieved in seniors' golf. In 2002 she won 11 tournaments on the LPGA Tour plus two more on the European Tour.

- Lorena Ochoa is the new world number one. The elegant Mexican won eight tournaments in 2007 including the British Women's Open. In 2008 she won four tournaments in a row on the LPGA Tour. In just five years she has amassed over $12.5 million in prize money.

These superstars are incredible sportswomen and it's an insult to their skill and talent to compare their golf to the exhibition-style play that's on show on the seniors' tours.

Now this may be a little superficial, but it's an important consideration for the purposes of this debate. Which is the more aesthetically pleasing prospect, a three-ball of 20-something women who are physically fit and stylishly dressed, or a group of balding, pot-bellied 50-something men waddling and wheezing their way around the course in 40-inch-waist pleated trousers and polo shirts so large a small family could camp in one? If you can honestly say the latter then you probably ought to seek help.

It's around the greens where the top females really display their skill. Watch any women's tournament and you'll see an incredible standard of pitching and putting – good enough to rival the top men. Watching the seniors on the greens is like accidentally tuning in to an endless teleshopping broadcast promoting broom-handle and belly putters. Seeing a normal-length blade is a rare event indeed in seniors' golf: 'What's that he's using there, Hank?' 'I'm not sure, Kent. It looks like one of those old-fashioned hands-and-arms putters.'

So it's stylish and attractive women playing incredible golf at the zenith of their careers versus overweight and unattractive old men enjoying a final fling to earn some extra beer money. There's no contest really.

39

MEDAL ROUND vs
BOUNCE GAME

Some people play golf as a purely recreational game while others view it as an ultra-competitive sport. Which camp has it right? Should we focus our attentions on winning the medal and lowering our handicap or just going out and enjoying the banter?

MEDAL ROUND

Golf is a sport. Many people enjoy it on a solely social level and that's fine. But first and foremost it's a sport where players compete against the course and each other, trying to better previous performances or outplay an opponent.

The competitive aspect of golf is one of its most appealing facets. Striving to beat a score is what makes people go back to the links. The medal is the best way of testing yourself in a truthful manner. When your name and score are up on the results board for all to see, you're forced to be truthful about your game.

When there's nothing to play for, golf can become boring. Just chapping it round with a few pals is not exactly a challenge. The medal round is the ultimate test – yes, it can be intimidating but there are few things more rewarding in the game than a well-constructed medal round. It gives you a buzz. The nerves jangle on the 1st tee, the 3-footers seem more like 10 and your heart is in your mouth as you play a final approach towards a packed clubhouse. It's a thrilling challenge.

When you complete a successful medal round people will come up to you to offer their congratulations: 'I heard you had a nett 67 in the spring meeting last week. Great shooting.' You'll feel proud of yourself and may even have a trophy to show for it. Nobody really cares how you get on in a bounce game. You're unlikely to be accosted in the locker room by someone saying, 'Hey, aren't you the chap who scored 37 Stableford points in your weekly knock-around last Sunday?'

The medal offers great camaraderie. Turn up on a Saturday and battle round your home course with friends, acquaintances or maybe just someone you've met on the day. Back in the clubhouse everyone will be discussing the pin position on the 14th or the state of the bunker to the right of the 6th. It's a great way to become involved in the club. If you don't play in the medal you're missing out.

Another good thing about medal rounds is that they count for handicap. A game is much more exciting and demanding when your handicap is on the line. The lip-out on the 2nd could mean you miss the buffer zone by one; the birdie at the last could mean a 0.2 cut. It should be every golfer's aim to get their handicap as low as they possibly can. To do this they must play regular medals. If you only step out a couple of times a year, you'll have no chance of getting cut as you'll put too much pressure on yourself.

Would you bother going to a casino that uses only Monopoly money? OK, you might have a good time playing the tables but there'd be no element of risk, no adrenalin surge. Sometimes you just want to take a chance. This is what the medal round delivers – a chance to cut your handicap, a chance of glory and a chance of excitement.

BOUNCE GAME

You might think we've been here before in the medal vs Stableford debate. But whereas that one was all about which is the preferable competitive format, this one simply asks whether competitive formats are a wise option at all. If you wish to maintain a handicap you should, and indeed must, embark on a modest competitive schedule – perhaps once a month. But on those other three weekends it's far better to keep things friendly.

This isn't to do with those misguided anti-competition senti-ments advocated by modern educationalists. In today's schools the notion of 'top of the class' is a complete taboo while the parents' sack race has been banned for fear of the lifelong emotional trauma little Johnny might suffer if he has to watch his old man trounced by Timmy's dad. All utter tosh of course, for competition pervades all areas of modern society. Deprive someone of it and they may not know how to survive in the real world.

Are you putting in enough hours in the race for promotion with Simpson from accounts? Are your house and car keeping up with the Joneses'? Is there a credit card with a lower interest rate to relieve the burden of your overspending? The list is endless. And because the rest of life is so competitive, why would you want to add golf into the cut-and-thrust mix too?

The problem is that everything you say or do counts either for or against you in life's hard-fought race. If you let that mentality spill over into your weekend golf, where is your escape, your regular pit stop to refuel with life's real values of friendship, camaraderie and, yes, even laughter?

There's certainly no room for laughter in the monthly medal, and little room for banter once everyone is in that 'must beat my handicap; mustn't go up 0.1' tunnel-vision mindset. Yes, we might be playing with friends, but that friendship is barely of relevance as we set our sights single-mindedly on our competitive goals for the day.

In the bounce game, it's just you and your golfing chums having fun together. Self-deprecation and mickey-taking are the order of the day as the golf itself takes secondary importance to the good time you're all having after another gruelling week grafting away for your family's future.

'Does your husband play?' someone chirps up as you leave a 15-footer 6 feet short. Making the same comment in a medal would be a major faux pas, met with silence and frosty glares that say, *There's nothing funny about this; if I miss that one I've got no chance of playing to handicap and this will have been a complete waste of my precious time!*

No, the medal round is too much like hard work, and as we know, all work and no play makes Jack a dull boy. So stick to the bounce game if you don't want to be thought a dullard who can only ever function when there's something on the line.

That's not a caddie - that's his tax adviser.

40
ELITE AMATEUR vs JOURNEYMAN PROFESSIONAL

So you've got more than a bit of talent for the game? What do you do? Work your way up through the amateur ranks to see just how far you can get playing merely for pride, or venture into golf's paid ranks where the harsh reality is that relatively few will make it to the very top and the majority will forever remain mere journeymen?

ELITE AMATEUR

The supremely talented 18-year-old golfer has a decision to make – turn professional and try to earn a living from the game, or remain an elite amateur, keeping options open.

In recent years many excellent young amateur golfers have opted for the former, tempted by contracts from sports management firms. The instant cash on the table must be a considerable lure but, for many, taking the plunge has been to the detriment of their playing careers.

It's phenomenally difficult to break into the very top echelon of professional golf, and competition to play in, let alone win, the biggest money events is intense. There are numerous solid touring pros who've never quite made it to the pinnacle of the paid ranks and find themselves scratching a living on one of the many tours across the globe. These 'journeymen' have a pressured and often unprofitable existence.

The life of a journeyman pro is a juggling act. Spending weeks away from home, travelling the world on a shoestring, knowing only a top-20 finish will see them break even for the week. They play in strange countries with few spectators watching their efforts, in a desperate attempt to earn enough cash to make next year's schedule more bearable or avoid a visit to the dreaded tour school.

Many journeymen rue the day they chose to forego their amateur status, particularly as today's elite amateurs enjoy such charmed lives. Make it to the top of the amateur game in the UK and your national golf union will treat you like royalty. The English, Scottish, Welsh and Irish elite squads receive instruction from the top coaches, advice from psychologists and fitness experts plus plenty of equipment. For a journeyman pro to get such support, he'd have to spend half his yearly winnings.

In the UK, amateur tournaments visit some of the country's most prestigious courses. In 2009, the Amateur championship was played over the links at Formby, the Brabazon Trophy was contested at Moortown and the Links Trophy was once again at St Andrews. Now look at the Europro Tour by comparison; pros on that satellite circuit have experienced the likes of the Marriott at Tudor Park and Wychwood Park through 2009.

As an elite amateur you're not committed to golf. You can still pursue your education or another career path. If, when it comes to the crunch, you decide playing golf for a living isn't for you, then you'll still have other options. Moving into the pro ranks you must fully commit your life to playing golf in order to achieve success. A few years down that road and you'll be struggling to see other available avenues.

If you're not yet convinced it's preferable to be a top amateur than a middle-of-the-road pro, consider this finally – would you rather become British Amateur Champion and join a roll-call of victors including Bobby Jones, Sir Michael Bonallack and Peter McEvoy? Or would you prefer to pick up a few thousand euros for victory in the Telenet Trophy on the Challenge Tour joining illustrious winners like Toni Karjalainen and Nicolas Vanhootegem?

If it's the latter, good luck at tour school.

JOURNEYMAN PROFESSIONAL

For most of us, work will form a somewhat inconvenient obstacle to more pleasurable pursuits for the best part of 40 years. But if the opportunity to combine the two were to arise, offering you the chance to earn a more-than-decent crust doing something you love, who in their right mind would turn it down?

Such is the lot of the so-called journeyman professional – someone able to make a comfortably adequate living from his golfing ability, even if never threatening to become one of the sport's millionaire superstars.

But what exactly constitutes a journeyman? A Europro Tour hopeful; a habitual Challenge Tour competitor who never quite makes the grade; or someone consistently in the lower reaches of the main European Tour? For most, it is the last of these – someone you wouldn't physically know from Adam, but whose name you half know from scrolling through the scores every week; someone likely to be involved in the scrap for tour survival come season's end; someone like England's Robert Rock, who burst onto the scene in 2003, but who until 2009 had never really made much of a mark.

A failure. Someone destined to never quite make it. That would be a typical assessment of Rock and his ilk. But look again at the figures. Even when he finished between 111th and 177th on the Order of Merit for five consecutive years, he still averaged €167,000 (roughly £145,000) a year. Even taking his considerable expenses into account, that's still way in excess of the national average wage of around £25,000 for doing something he loves doing. The elite amateur, on the other hand, goes through pretty much the same process during the season, but in return for his golfing talent banks nothing more than prestige and honour, while still racking up hefty expenses.

Yes, there must be days when it all seems too much like hard work for the journeyman. But not as hard as, say, for a miner, or even a salesman just presented with 'not-a-cat-in-hell's-chance' targets. And there must be far more days when he has to pinch himself to confirm that, yes, people are indeed paying him to do something most would happily pay to do.

To finish, a quick look back at the 2009 Irish Open, where the difference between elite amateur and journeyman professional was brought sharply into focus. Shane Lowry, an Irish amateur playing in his first tour event, amazingly won the title in a play-off. And who did he beat? None other than Robert Rock, for whom 2009 proved the year his journey finally gathered momentum. Lowry, for all his efforts in the worst of the Irish weather, walked away with a trophy and the admiration of some enthusiastic home fans; Rock walked away with 500,000 euros – the amount Lowry would have pocketed had his amateur status not prevented him from receiving prize money.

And that is the thing with the journeyman – the journey itself brings a comfortable lifestyle, with always just a hope that eventually it might lead somewhere better. Surely that's reason enough to give it a go, however disparagingly dismissive others may be of those a couple of rungs down professional golf's lofty ladder?

Ben Hogan

41
LONG IRON vs UTILITY CLUB

The man who can strike a pure 2-iron off a tight lie commands immediate respect from his golfing peers. He achieves something approaching godlike status among his regular playing partners. But, for the average punter, is a long iron the sensible option? Wouldn't most golfers benefit from making the switch to a forgiving utility club?

LONG IRON

The death of the long iron and the rise of the utility club is one of golf's greatest tragedies. Throughout the twentieth century golfers who could clip a 2-iron off a tight lie were put on a pedestal. The skill should still be the benchmark by which golfing ability is measured. Unfortunately any old hacker can now move it a good distance from the fairway, or even the rough, by purchasing a ridiculous-looking contraption resembling a baby's shoe on the end of a stick. The utility club is embarrassing and detrimental to our sport.

You can shape the ball with a long iron, curve it round a tree or chase it up to a pin tucked in the back left corner of a green. The principal function of the utility club is to get the ball airborne. It does this effectively, but beyond that its virtues are limited. The ball flight from a utility club is high, weak and difficult to manipulate. The shot shape is extremely unsatisfying to behold and totally useless in any sort of wind.

The feeling of a purely struck long-iron shot is unrivalled in golf. Nipping the ball perfectly from the top of the turf and watching it fizz away low and straight sets the pulse racing and makes the hairs on the back of the neck stand up. Yes, it's a difficult skill to master but a mightily rewarding one once you have the hang of it. If you choose to buy your way to a good long game through the use of utility clubs you're a coward and are opting out. It's the equivalent of learning to drive an automatic car because it's too hard to work out how to operate a manual shift. You'll still get from A to B but the experience will be far less fun. If you'd stuck it out and learned how to do it the proper way you'd have gained more self-assurance and earned more respect.

Which of the following is the more memorable and admirable image: Ben Hogan's majestic 1-iron to the final green of the US Open at Merion in 1950, or Todd Hamilton scrambling his way round Troon and using a utility club for nearly every shot to win the 2004 Open? The former conjures romantic images of legends of the sport from a more elegant age. The latter, one of the most disappointing Open championships in history, represented the worst aspects of golf's technological advances – those that have levelled the playing field and allowed lesser players to compete against, and beat, superior golfers. As utility club technology was advancing, Nick Price (one of golf's best iron players) was quoted as saying he felt he'd lost a unique advantage over his peers. Sadly the trend applies to the amateur game as well. Duffers who, by rights, shouldn't be able to compete due to their inept techniques can muddle through because of the forgiving nature of utility clubs. It's unfair, unsporting and just not golf.

UTILITY CLUB

This one really is what our American friends would term a no-brainer.

Can you relate to this? You get a decent drive away on a par 5 and find yourself 210 yards out. You know you can just about get home, or certainly pretty close, if you flush your 3-iron. The lie's OK but not great, perhaps sitting down a little more than you'd ideally like. You get ready to play, but as you look down the club head seems to visibly shrink. There's little apparent loft to help you send the ball up and away, so you tense up a little, spending too long frozen over the ball for your own good. Your mind starts to play tricks – was that a little breeze in your face? You'll really have to step on it now to get it there. And even the slightest hint of club striking turf before ball will take yards off your shot.

It is at precisely this moment of maximum mental turmoil that your body decides almost involuntarily to commence the swing. Everything happens in a blur. Rather than the smooth tempo you need to sweep a crisp long iron away, your body performs some kind of contorted high-speed lunge – the very antithesis of rhythm – and your ball squirts away low and right into the thick clag well off the fairway. From a potential birdie-making position you're now into damage limitation mode, trying to salvage what you can from the hole while simultaneously ignoring an overactive brain that won't let you forget just what a fool you are for wasting another perfect drive.

If only there were another way. Thankfully there is: the utility club – long-game saviour of both amateur and professional alike. Golf's one cardinal equipment sin is not having at least one of these nifty little numbers in your bag at all times. They've transformed the long game from nigh-on impossible to readily achievable for mere golfing mortals and from tough to straightforward for the game's elite who have been ditching their longest irons in droves for golf's new wonder clubs. Doesn't that tell you all you need to know?

So just how are they imbued with such magical properties? Well, their mini-wood head designs boast shallow faces and wide rounded soles that ensure plenty of weight is below the equator of the ball at impact, to help you get the ball up and away with ease and provide far greater forgiveness on heavier strikes. And with shaft lengths closer to those of irons, they also promise greater control than fairway woods. They really are the complete, all-round long-game package.

And it doesn't stop there either. With a little practice and imagination they can also be used in a variety of other situations, from playing out of thickish rough where long irons are a real no-go, to chipping out from under trees or even around the greens.

So what would you rather have in your bag – one of these versatile, multi-talented little clubs, or a cantankerous, mean-looking long iron? It isn't even close.

42

VERY SLOW GREENS vs
VERY FAST GREENS

The putting surfaces of Britain vary greatly from course to course, such that the average golfer will face many different green speeds over a season. Occasionally he'll encounter, and have to adapt to, greens that are either exceptionally sluggish or ridiculously fast. But which are the tougher to putt on – super-slow or super-slick?

VERY SLOW GREENS

Most golfers play on mid-paced greens for most of the year so develop putting strokes to suit them. This means anything other than mid pace will require certain adjustments. As to whether very slow or very fast greens are harder to putt on, the choice really is between a woolly shagpile carpet and a pristine, slick billiard table. Put it in those terms and it's hard to understand why anyone would find the latter tougher. It's not quite such a foregone conclusion, of course, with many struggling to adapt to lightning surfaces. But the truth is, those cursedly slow greens are more likely to test your powers of adaptability to the limit for three critical reasons.

The first, obviously, is that you have to hit the ball harder than usual. For most of us, trying to hit it harder with a full golf swing leads to loss of control and random results, and it's exactly the same with the putter. Extending the backswing just that bit further and then bringing the club back to the ball with greater force opens the door to miscues as we fail to time it properly, striking the ball inconsistently with the putter face too open or too closed. This inevitably results in bigger misses, and therefore more three-putts than with the more compact, easy-to-control putting action we're used to. By comparison, fast greens can be a godsend because so much less can go wrong directionally when you're only taking the putter back a very short way.

The other two reasons stem from the same root cause – an inability to mentally override what the eye sees in terms of pace and line. With regard to pace, nowhere is this truer than on the downhiller, where your eyes will be telling your brain that you've just got to breathe on this to get it there. But on desperately slow greens this is not the case, with the longer grass severely neutralising the effects of the slope so that you can hit it much more firmly than you might ever imagine. Of course, once you've left the first putt short you've then got to go through the whole process again. And just how long does it take your dozy brain to realise it's being led astray by your eyes? Usually until the 18th green.

Then there's the little matter of any break a putt may have. We just can't get it into our heads that the ball won't break as much as normal because it's subject to greater frictional resistance from the grass. So we invariably allow too much for the break and miss on the high side.

No one is saying that fast greens are a pushover for anyone not used to them. They can be quite frightening for a few holes until you adapt. But adapt you will, and come the end of the round you'll be reaping their full benefits to such an extent that you'll already have mentally drafted a letter to your greens committee demanding the mower blades be set a little lower at your home club. Conversely, you'll never find anyone pleading for snail's-pace greens, which tells you all you need to know, doesn't it?

VERY FAST GREENS

Do you prefer driving when the roads are warm, dry and grippy or when they're cold, icy and slippery? With the former you have total control over your vehicle and can drive fast with confidence. With the latter you're on a constant knife-edge. If you're careful, you can negotiate the route safely, but the slightest lapse in concentration or the smallest hint of over-aggression can lead to disaster.

A comparison between putting on slow and fast greens may not be this extreme or life-threatening but there are similarities. On slow greens you are in complete control of your ball's fate; you can putt with aggression and certainty. On overly fast greens you must be extremely tentative and, even then, you can be caught out by a surface that's beyond your control. Slopes can make the speed so severe that it's almost impossible to get your putts close to the hole.

For those of a delicate disposition when it comes to putting, nothing is more terrifying than a lightning-fast green. No matter how close to the hole you get, you can never be totally confident of sending the ball into the centre of the cup. You know that even the merest break or slightest push or pull of the blade will send the ball careering off-line, causing a complete miss or dreaded lip-out.

A lip-out on any green is one of the most frustrating moments in golf. The ball seems headed for the safe confines of the cup but, at the last moment, it moves ever so slightly off-line and hits the edge. It skirts round the back like a gravity-defying roller coaster before slinging out of the hole and away. It's infuriating. The irritation of a lip-out is exacerbated by overly fast greens. Not only will you have missed the putt but the ball will have accelerated as it travels around the rim of the hole and will have ended up 3 or 4 feet away, leaving another tester on the way back.

You have to hit the ball that bit harder on a slow green but, for most, this is a good thing as it eliminates one of the major causes of poor putting among amateur golfers – deceleration. Slowing the putter head down as it comes back towards the ball is extremely destructive and can lead to that appalling affliction, the yips. It's a condition all too common amongst amateurs who have to face the rigours of fast greens week in, week out. Those who play on slower greens are far more confident on the short grass as they're used to having to give the ball a bit of a rap to get it up to the cup. When they travel to a course with quicker greens, it may take them a little time to adapt to the speed but their stroke will be sound and, when they do get to grips with the pace, they'll putt with conviction and self-belief.

43

DRIVING RANGE vs CLUB PRACTICE GROUND

'I really ought to practise more' is a common lament among golfers. Yes, in order to improve we would all benefit from spending a little time hitting balls. But where is the best place to do it – from a comfortable covered bay at a busy driving range, or down at the club's practice ground in splendid isolation?

DRIVING RANGE

Pure convenience means the driving range stands head and shoulders above the club practice ground. You pull into the car park, grab your sticks from the boot, saunter in, hit a bucket of balls from a covered (sometimes heated) bay and leave. The whole process needn't take more than half an hour – perfect for the busy golfer looking to fit a spot of practice into his schedule.

In contrast, a trip to the practice ground can be a monumental undertaking. You ask in the pro shop if anyone's using the facility. 'Nope' is the confident answer, so you set off. It takes 20 minutes to cross the three fairways between car park and practice ground as a ladies' match is in full flow. When you reach the barely mown strip of field that passes for your practice area you find someone firing balls down from the other end. You curse under your breath and sit down in the shade of a tree.

Half an hour later he finally leaves, so you get your chance. But after 15 minutes of hitting the pro suddenly appears with a group of juniors for their weekly coaching session. You feel like a scolded child as you trudge around collecting your balls (you can only find 26 of the 40 you took down). To add insult to injury, it starts to rain as you make your way back to the clubhouse.

Good modern driving ranges have a multitude of targets to aim at – greens, flags, even water hazards. There are distance markers at regular intervals so you get a clear indication of how far you're hitting each club. Many ranges have soft-strike mats to replicate the feeling of grass and some even allow you to pay extra to play from real turf.

On the practice ground you've nothing to aim at and nothing to help with distances. Unless you pace out 100, 150 and 200 yards and stick poles in the ground, you'll be firing off shots without any sensible objective.

Another thing that helps you gauge relative distances at the range is the consistency of the balls. OK, they might not be Pro V1s but most ranges now have decent, new balls of the same brand. In the average practice bag there'll be an incredible hotchpotch of old balls – beat-up Titleist balatas to Top-Flite Magnas. How are you supposed to find any sort of consistency practising with balls that vary in feel from Play-Doh to granite?

A good driving range generally has a pro shop attached. If you're in the market for a new piece of equipment you can get advice from the pro before taking demo models on to the range to trial. It's by far the most sensible way to purchase new kit.

You can go to the range with a group of people of varying abilities. The more competent players can get some much-needed practice. The beginners can start to get a feel for how to play the game in a safe environment without condescending members raising eyebrows every time they fail to get the ball airborne.

Yes, this one is straightforward. It's driving range by a landslide.

CLUB PRACTICE GROUND

If you practise once a week and the average basket of range balls costs £4 or £5, the first incentive for choosing the practice ground over the driving range is one of stark economics – an extra £200 to £250 in your pocket at the end of the year. That's enough for a nice new driver or a year's supply of top-notch balls, with some left over for a handy little sweetener for the other half.

But there are other benefits beyond the financial savings. On the practice ground you get to choose what balls you use. At the range you'll often have to hit poor-quality balls foisted on you by penny-pinching owners, or ones that only fly 75 per cent of full distance because the range has been built on too small a plot. Who really wants to see a flushed 7-iron just scrape past the 100-yard marker, or a full-blooded drive leave the end fence untroubled? OK, you may not have to pick the balls up, but you're then missing out on the chance to a) see how long and accurate your shots really were, and b) hone your wedge keepy-uppy skills to impress your mates.

On the practice ground you'll often play off real grass, the very surface on which the game is played. An unyielding synthetic mat tells you nothing about how club interacts with turf at impact, and the danger is you'll end up only ever picking the ball cleanly off the surface rather than driving down and through.

At the range you're likely to be sandwiched between some overweight meat-head who can't comprehend how your controlled swing hits it further than his wild lunge, and the novice from hell who occasionally sends one ricocheting off the roof, pinball-style, into your bay. More likely than not, there'll be a group lesson conducted by a cocky trainee pro called Wayne who is attempting, but failing, to get across the basics of the swing in language even total beginners can grasp. The practice ground, on the other hand, is reserved for members and visitors who can usually at least hit it forwards. And you'll often enjoy blissful solitude, allowing you to work on your game in peace.

Serious practisers will have a bag of cast-off balls no longer quite up to on-course duty, yet perfectly fine for practice, keeping feel off the face constant. They'll mark their balls in a unique way – much like the graffiti artist's tag – so if they do have to share the facilities, they'll still walk off with the same number of balls they started with. And in the exclusive brotherhood of practice-ground users, everyone knows everyone else's tags, so the odd stray will invariably find its way home – a kind of unwritten code of practice-ground etiquette.

I suppose ranges win in winter when, for most people, practice is confined to the hours of darkness. But who really wants to spend an hour watching their own breath on a freezing range when they could be down a cosy pub talking through their hopes for the golfing year ahead with their mates?

44
CHIP AND RUN vs
LOB SHOT

The lofted parachute shot that lands like a feather on silly putty or the perfectly weighted runner that rolls out to the hole edge, leaving just a tap-in? When executed correctly both are highly satisfying, but which is the superior and more versatile shot . . .?

CHIP AND RUN

The flop shot is a recent invention brought about by the emergence of American-style target courses. We've been conned by equipment manufacturers that the high looping shot is the most suitable option when we're anywhere near the green. Why? Because we'll need a unique item of equipment to achieve the parachute shot – the lob wedge. It's a marketing scam.

The thing is, there are relatively few courses in the UK where a lob shot is more appropriate than the reliable chip and run. The hard and fast links certainly demand a lower pitch. The running chip is also more appropriate on heathland courses that become bare and firm through the summer months. In fact, there are very few courses in Britain watered so extensively that their greens remain soft in midsummer. Hard putting surfaces make the lob a very unpredictable shot to attempt, so during the British summer it's basically obsolete.

The chip and run is not only the most effective shot around Britain's greens, it's also the safest. Judging a chip and run wrong you might be left with a longer putt than expected. Get the lob shot wrong and you're in a whole heap of trouble. You'll either catch the ball thin, flying it eight times as far as you'd expected (probably into a pond or out of bounds), or you'll 'dunch' it. Decelerating into the ball and catching the ground first, you'll move it about 5 feet, possibly making contact twice.

A key advantage of the chip and run becomes apparent when it comes to your next shot. More often than not you'll fail to get your chip or pitch stone-dead however you play it, so you'll be left with a putt to save par or bogey. If you've played a chip and run your ball will have rolled across a good portion of the green. This will give you a valuable insight into the slopes on the putting surface and an indication of its speed. If you play a well-executed lob shot, it should stop pretty much wherever it lands, giving you no indication of how fast or sloping the green is.

The lob shot is the Lamborghini of pitches – flashy and liable to draw oohs and aahs from those who witness it in all its glory. Yet it's often costly and, with it, you always feel you're teetering on the verge of things going horribly wrong. In contrast the chip and run is an Audi – understated and modest yet supremely reliable. It will continue to perform year after year. It'll never break down and will require very little maintenance. In a sport that requires consistency and prudence, these assets are by far the more practical.

Of course there are situations that demand an attempt at a high-flighted pitch – when you must carry a bunker or water hazard and stop the ball quickly on the other side. But these scenarios are the exception rather than the rule. Any connoisseur of the game will recognise just how functional the chip and run is. It's the classic British shot. Master it and you'll be getting up and down more often than not.

LOB SHOT

Some pundits would say that the canniest golfers are those who get the ball on the ground and running as soon as possible around the greens and, to be fair, when circumstances allow they may be right.

But what happens when circumstances most decidedly do not allow, and those dastardly course designers have inconsiderately seen fit to put obstacles between you and the flag that render the chip and run a non-starter? This will happen quite often if they've done their job properly and positioned their cunning greenside mounds, bunkers, hollows and ponds at the points of 'most likely miss'. What happens then when the option of the chip and run is taken off the table? Basically you're snookered, unless you've mastered the ambitious chaser through the sand, or the pond-skimming Barnes Wallis à la Masters competitors at Augusta's 16th on practice days.

In such scenarios, if the high lob is missing from your golfing CV, the likely outcomes include the sickening bullet-like thin that's still rising when it clears the out-of-bounds fence beyond the green, or the demoralising duff into the terrifying bunker you'd been so anxious to avoid on your approach – quite possibly somewhere up the face, tucked under its Mick Jaggeresque lip.

Yes, have the chip and run at your disposal by all means, but it is mastery of the lob shot that will better equip you to avoid those heart-sinking big numbers when you get badly out of position around the greens. High-floating, soft-landing lobs can get you out of trouble where chip and runs fear to tread. With the right wedge line-up, you may even be able to play them off tight lies too rather than just the more accommodating fluffy ones, as long as you're suitably positive through impact and steer clear of the dreaded deceleration of doom.

Because lobs don't run much on landing, they offer greater scope for precise control by taking the vagaries of the bounce out of the equation – the one thing that can all too easily derail even the most well-thought-out and executed chip and run. In most instances the lob has only one telling bounce, and that will be on the green, so it should prove fairly predictable. If your chip and run takes just one wayward bounce at the wrong moment on its journey across sometimes uneven terrain, you can be made to look rather stupid, especially if you catch a swale or crest that wouldn't have come into play with a straight bounce. Missing by miles when supposedly playing safe will leave your mates distinctly unimpressed; executing a perfect Phil Mickelson lob when you'd looked dead and buried will have them hailing you as the next short-game demigod.

So study Phil's technique carefully, practise extensively away from the course, then treat your friends to a lob shot masterclass next time they take you on. They'll probably be more in awe of you than if you'd blitzed a 350-yarder straight down the middle – and more importantly, every missed green will hold less fear for you.

Nick Faldo   Seve Ballesteros

45

FALDO vs
SEVE

*After a decade in the doldrums, the 1980s witnessed the return of
Europe to the forefront of world golf. Two men spearheaded this revival
– a feisty, impetuous Spaniard called Severiano Ballesteros and a master
of the technical and tactical called Nick Faldo. On course they were like
chalk and cheese, but who was the better golfer?*

FALDO

To choose between Seve and Faldo is to choose between swash-
buckling heroism and methodical calculation. But where many
would normally lean towards the former for largely romantic
reasons, in this instance they would be wrong to do so.

These two players have been Europe's most prolific major winners of the modern era, with Faldo just pipping Seve 6–5. But that isn't the reason for siding with Faldo. While Seve was performing unlikely heroics and, quite frankly, getting away with murder, Faldo was shrewd and brave enough to realise that what he had – good though it was – simply wasn't good enough to make him a regular major contender. He knew he needed a more reliable swing to better withstand the pressure of coming down the stretch with one of golf's biggest titles on the line.

So he sought out David Leadbetter and underwent one of the most dramatic 'before and after' swing changes of any top player – a bold statement of intent far braver than any of Seve's miracle recoveries if you look at the bigger picture.

The result was that even though both are a similar age, Seve's major-winning river had dried up by the 1988 Open while Faldo was just embarking on a journey to five major titles in six years, and six in a decade. His 1996 Masters victory was the icing on the cake at a time when Seve had ceased to be a factor in golf's big four.

Yes, Faldo irritated us with his fidgety mannerisms, his aloofness, his sometimes ill-chosen words and his occasional high-profile flare-ups with the press. But oh, how we loved him in 1989 and 1990 when he made the second Sunday in April one of the most thrilling nights of the year as he claimed back-to-back Green Jackets. Even better that his two play-off victims were cussed awkward Scott Hoch and swaggering Ray Floyd!

But what really elevates Faldo above Seve is the wisdom with which he has chosen to depart top-level competitive golf. He knew when the game was up; prior to his retirement in 2007, you sensed right to the end of his career that Seve still felt he had another major in him. Faldo was of course right to gracefully slip into other golfing roles; Seve's long-winded departure was cantankerous and anything but graceful, so that he alienated himself a little from his once-adoring fans. Meanwhile, Faldo's fan base has grown with his new-found role as commentator and analyst.

Faldo knew the writing was on the wall a few years ago and didn't try to fight it kicking and screaming as Seve did. For Faldo it probably happened at the 2003 Open when a front-nine eagle on Sunday got him right into the thick of it. He crumbled on the back nine, but marched up the 18th fairway when he could no longer win, looking rather too pleased with his top-ten finish for a man who truly believed he could still compete at the highest level. The Faldo of old would have been disgusted at letting such an opportunity slip away.

So Faldo truly is the classier act, not so much for his superior major record as for the realism with which he accepted that his heyday as a player was over.

SEVE

The flawed genius always has a special place in the hearts of the general public. George Best, James Dean and River Phoenix live on in the collective conscience as renegades who dared to be different. Their failings are quickly confined to the dustbin of history. Seve Ballesteros is not a hellraiser or a drug addict, but as far as golf goes he fits the flawed genius tag rather well. From his early days, learning with a 3-iron on the beach, his talent for golfing invention was apparent. He could play shots from his knees and bend the ball around, under or over trees. He could even make birdies from the car park! His feisty character and, at times, strange behaviour only served to nourish the mystique surrounding him.

If professional golfers were forced to find a new job, Seve's careers adviser would have given him two choices: pirate or magician. No player in the history of the game deserves the label of a swashbuckler as much as the man from Santander. It was his unpredictability that was so thrilling. You never knew what was coming next but you could bet it would be cavalier and courageous. At times he was spellbinding, his Houdini-like escapism defied belief. He entertained golf crowds throughout his career and is one of the most popular players of all time.

In contrast Nick Faldo would almost certainly go and become an accountant. He was a meticulous yet dreary golfer who ground down his opposition rather than dazzling them with his brilliance. Through the 1980s Faldo ironed out the flair in his game in favour of technical perfection. It was his dedication to technique and practice rather than inspiration and panache that won him six majors. He was, of course, a great champion with an unflinching determination to succeed. But he could never win the public's affection like his Spanish contemporary. Faldo lacked Seve's audacity and bravado. If you watched showreels of Seve and Faldo's greatest moments, the former would be considerably more entertaining.

In terms of playing careers there's little to separate the pair. Faldo won six majors to Ballesteros's five, but Seve's were won with incomparable style and drama. At one stage in the final round of the 1980 US Masters he led by ten, he construed to throw it away and his lead was pegged back to just two; he then pulled away again and won by four. What a showman! Seve won 50 titles on the European Tour; no player has won more. In the Ryder Cup he won 20 of his 37 matches (54 per cent); Faldo won 23 of 46 (50 per cent).

When you think of golf's most memorable moments, Seve will pop into your head more than once. The exuberant 19-year-old who burst kicking and screaming on to the scene with a second place in the 1976 Open at Birkdale; his fantastic fist-pumping celebration after holing the winning putt in the 1984 Open at St Andrews or driving the 10th green at the Belfry in the 1985 Ryder Cup. Seve captured the golfing world's imagination with his passionate zeal for the game. He's an icon.